THE STONEWORKER'S BIBLE

Dedication

This book is very respectfully dedicated to the pioneer stone cutters and setters whose stonework has written man's history in stone structures, both great and small.

No. 1226
$12.95

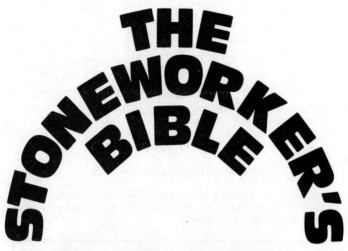

THE STONEWORKER'S BIBLE

BY J. M. NICKEY

TAB BOOKS

BLUE RIDGE SUMMIT, PA. 17214

FIRST EDITION

FIRST PRINTING—DECEMBER 1979

Copyright © 1979 by J.M. Nickey

Printed in the United States of America

Library of Congress Cataloging in Publication Data

Nickey, J.M.
    The stoneworker's bible.

    Includes index.
    1. Building, Stone—Handbooks, manuals, etc.
I. Title.
TH5401.N52   624'.1832   79-23430
ISBN 0-8306-9714-4
ISBN 0-8306-1226-2 pbk.

Contents

Introduction

The intent of this book is to make construction with stone more familiar to anyone who is interested in doing stonework without having to become indentured as an apprentice.

From the time man first set a stone in the mouth of a cave for a door, the art has advanced to modern methods of construction. During the construction of the stone walls of Mycenae, the Etruscan unsquared stone construction, the Cyclopean stonework in Greece and Italy, and the Gothic stonework work architecture, construction with stone reached a picturesque style and advancement.

Mortar was not used in Egyptian stonework. They wrought, polished, and set their stone so close in the stonework that the joints were hardly visible. Mortar came later and is used today.

Learning to set stone possibly started before the time of the master masons of Sienna, who had their own guild of masons and apprentices. Today the stonemason's union indentures an apprentice to give him a chance to learn the basic methods of constructing with stone.

There are many methods of construction, handling tools, mixing mortar formulas, and mortar handling that are centuries old but still used today. These procedures along with the contemporary additions of materials, high quality cements, limes and powered tools, will be used for years to come.

Comprehension is the reader's desire and this book's purpose. The person who reads and applies this practical knowledge will become proficiently artistic in constructing with stone.

I have included in this book many fundamental principles of stonework that I have practiced throughout my many years as a stonemason.

This book contains practical information on materials and quantities, along with methods to lay up finished stonework that will be sound, enduring and pleasing to the eye. Anyone who follows the instructions and procedures put forth in this book can, with practice, become proficient in stonework.

The knowledge pertaining to stonework presented in this book should assist the do-it-yourself builders and masonry contractors—even architects—to a more enlightened understanding of stonework construction.

J.M. Nickey

Chapter 1
Tools
and Equipment

It can be truly said that a stonemason has written "history in stone." From the time the first stone was set in the mouth of a cave as a door to the present time, the stone mason has constructed big and little buildings, from a mass of stone, for use and pleasure.

Stonemasons are capable of selecting, cutting, shaping, dressing and setting stone, whether natural or fabricated, with or without mortar. They can set stone in an ashlar, broken, random, or coursed pattern bond, whether neat, dressed or rustic, as well as in a riprap, cobble, rubble, ashlar or decorative design. They understand the basic methods of stonework construction, although there are procedures and artistic touches unique to each stonemason. Their works have proven them artisans. This book, if followed, can help any person become a proficient stonemason.

Many kinds of tools and equipment are needed when doing stonework. The use of several of these tools and pieces of equipment will be discussed and illustrated in this chapter as well as throughout the book.

Everyone will find certain methods best suited for them. And tools can be used by either the left or right-handed person. I have never seen a right or left-handed trowel. There are methods of procedure and artistic touches unique to each stonemason.

HAMMERS

There are various kinds and sizes of hammers needed for certain purposes in stonework. A claw hammer is used for driving

Fig. 1-1. Straight or bent claw hammers come in all sizes.

nails and pulling them out. It is a tool used throughout all kinds of building construction.

These claw hammers can be procured in various sizes and weights. They are made with either a straight claw or a bent, curved claw. Either type of claw hammer will do the same thing. It all depends on the workmen whether a straight claw or a bent claw is best for them or for the particular job they are doing. (Fig. 1-1)

Ax Hammer

The *ax hammer* is chisel-pointed on both edges, about 12 to 14 pounds in weight, and is used primarily for removing nobs or uneven projections left by the pick hammer. It is also used when dressing stone (Fig. 1-2).

The ax hammer comes in different sizes and weights. The lighter weights have shorter handles than do the heavier, larger size heads.

This hammer has wide, blunt chisel-like faces. It is used to cut stone apart. The ax hammer will generally halve a stone rather than

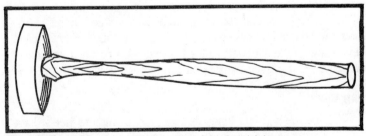

Fig. 1-2. The ax hammer removes nobs left by the pick hammer.

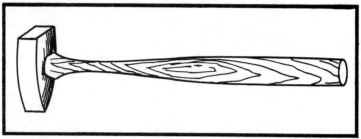

Fig. 1-3. A spalling hammer is effective when squaring stone.

shatter it. These halves will usually have to be further wrought to be usable in stonework.

Spalling Hammer

The *spalling hammer* has flat edges, with about 1½-inch square faces. It is used for knocking off rough lumps and for squaring stone. This hammer's head weighs from 12 to 14 pounds. (Fig. 1-3)

The spalling hammer is of various weights and sizes. The chisel face can be long or short. This hammer can be procured in a small size with a short handle. It is especially usable on small stones.

Mash Hammer

The *mash hammer*, whose head weighs from 2 to 5 pounds, is used on punches, chisels, sets, etc., when these items are used for wroughting (shaping or dressing) stone (Fig. 1-4).

Fig. 1-4. Mash hammers come in long and short handles.

Fig. 1-5. Combination bush and toothed ax hammers are excellent for wroughting stone to a finer face.

The hammer is used on larger stones, also. It is shown with a long, two-handed handle. It also comes with a short handle.

Combination Bush and Toothed Ax Hammer and Bolster

The small combination bush and toothed ax hammer is a good hammer for wroughting stone to a finer face (Fig. 1-5). This hammer is of two kinds. The heavy, long-handled hammer has both faces toothed and is used on large stones. The short-handled combination hammer has one flat toothed face and one curved chisel-shaped toothed face. This is a very handy hammer for use on smaller stones. It's a dandy hammer on softer stones.

The pick, with its 16 pound weight, is used for dressing and working, particularly granite, to within an inch of a finished face. It can also reduce fairly large stone to near its required shape (Fig. 1-6).

This *pick hammer* can stand considerable abuse. The pick faces are somewhat blunt. There is considerable bulk immediately back of its points. This hammer generally comes with a long handle.

Prospecting Hammer

The *prospecting hammer* is a handy hammer when making a pick-faced ashlar stone finish (Fig. 1-7). This prospecting hammer has one pointed pick face similar to the pick hammer, with the exception that the point face is longer and more delicate. Its other

12

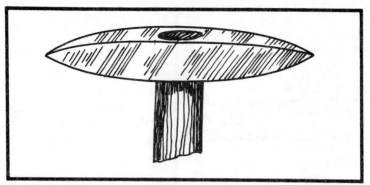

Fig. 1-6. A pick hammer is helpful when working on granite.

face is flat and square and can be used for doing shaping work on stones. It can also be used for pitching work.

Ax-like Hammer or Bolster

The ax-like hammer or bolster, is used for dressing (wroughting) down stone to an almost polished face. It is made with chisel plates bolted loosely together (Fig. 1-8).

The bolster is used for dressing down stone to a fine, almost smooth finish. Its blades are held apart by fillers. The blades are not held in a solid, tight position. They have freedom of movement which makes this hammer a top hammer for wroughting a finish on the face of stone.

Dummy and Mallets

The *dummy* weighing 4 pounds, is used for striking soft stone tools. It is made of zinc, lead or soft metal (Fig. 1-9). The dummy is

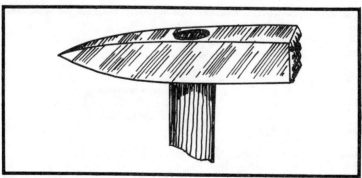

Fig. 1-7. The prospecting hammer can help make a pick-faced ashlar stone finish.

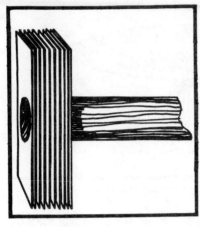

Fig. 1-8. Bolsters should be used when wroughting a finish.

also used to pound stone into place when it is being set. There are also round-headed hammers. These are smaller in weight and come in handy when setting patio or sidewalk stone tile.

The mallet with a rawhide core in each face, is used for striking sharp cutting chisels, punches, etc. (Fig. 1-10). This rawhide core hammer is also used when setting stone tile to pound the tile to place and alignment.

The hard rubber or wood mallet and regular mallet are used when tapping stone to proper place when setting it (Fig. 1-11). The rubber or wood mallet is a good one for larger stone tapping. It will not mar the stone face when used.

CHISELS AND CUTTING TOOLS

Chisels and hand-cutting tools are used in combination with various hammers, especially the mash hammer and mallets. These tools have long or short handles.

Fig. 1-9. The dummy hammers stone into place.

Fig. 1-10. A mallet is ideal for tapping chisels or punches.

The bladed chisel can be had in various sizes of blade widths. It is used for cutting and groomings on stone faces (Fig. 1-12).

This blade chisel is a hard-tempered chisel. It can stand hard use. The chisel can cut granite stone and the hardest concrete.

It comes in different weights and widths and can be bought with either short or long handles. The handles are of metal, not of wood or other material. This chisel, like other hand-held chisels, can be sharpened if care is taken not to overheat it during the sharpening process. The chisel is tempered too hard for a file to sharpen it. An emery power-driven wheel is best to use when sharpening a tool.

The Point

The *point* is used in combination with a hammer when wroughting (Fig. 1-13). Points are of different weights, sizes and handle

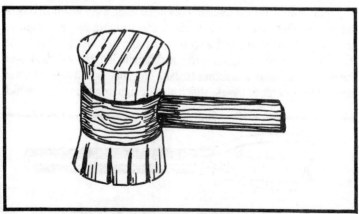

Fig. 1-11. This mallet will not damage stone faces.

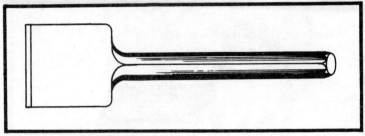

Fig. 1-12. The blade chisel is very durable.

lengths. They are used with a hammer during the process of wroughting stone.

Stone Bit

The stone bit is used when drilling holes in stone (Fig. 1-14).

This bit comes in long or short handles which are of different heights and sizes. It is held by one hand and tapped with a hammer. During the tapping, the bit is turned. This moving of the bit will enhance its cutting ability when tapped.

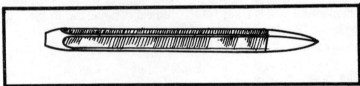

Fig. 1-13. A point works nice in conjunction with a hammer when wroughting.

Chisel-Type Tools

The numerous chisel-like tools have their uses when wroughting stone. They are of various sizes and weights and are used on small and large stone and also on hard and soft stone (Fig. 1-15).

The different weights, sizes, and handle lengths will designate the weight and size of hammer to use. The chisels and sets depicted are of different hardnesses, which also designates the uses to which

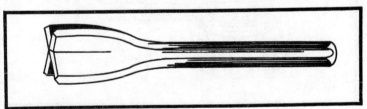

Fig. 1-14. Stone bits help to drill holes in stone.

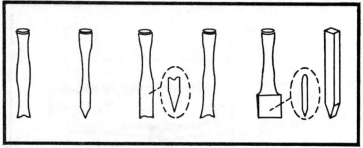

Fig. 1-15. These chisel-like tools are used on all kinds of stone.

they are put. Hard ones are generally used with care, as they are brittle and will break or chip off at their points or blades by rough usage.

One set comes in heavy, tough steel and can stand hard usage. This is a good set for pitching hard or soft stone.

The pencil-like chisel can have either a wide or narrow point. It is likened to a cold chisel and can be used on practically all stones.

Stone Cutter

The stone cutter is a semi-powered stone cutter operated with a hammer (Fig. 1-16). Some stone cutters are built for heavy stone and some for the smaller stone. They all can be used when cutting soft or hard stone. Different weight hammers can be used. This depends on the size of the cutter as well as the size of stone to be cut.

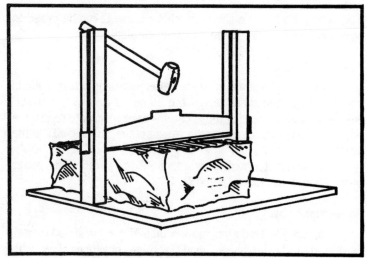

Fig. 1-16. This stone cutter is operated with a hammer.

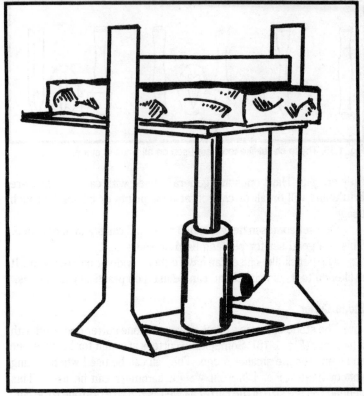

Fig. 1-17. The power stone cutter is hydraulic-powered.

The cutting blade has a sharp-chisel-like edge. It can be raised to accommodate any size stone within its capacity.

Power Stone Cutter

This hydraulic-powered stone cutter is a dandy. It is made in various sizes. The table moves the stone up against the chisel-sharpened blade. Some of these cutters have springs to return the table. This one returns due to the weight of the cutter itself and the stone.

The power stone cutter is a hydraulic-powered stone cutter operated with the foot (Fig. 1-17).

Power Stone Saw

A motor-powered stone saw comes in various sizes. It uses fabricated saw blades and diamond saw blades of various sizes, with a movable table, and makes clean cuts when cutting stone.

The saw in Fig. 1-18 is powered by an electric motor. There are other stone cutting saws powered by fuel engine. These saws have the blade lowered by a foot pedal. The stone is placed on the movable table, shifted to where it is to be cut, and the table is pushed toward the saw to cut the stone. There generally is a water pump which sits in the water in the frame reservoir. The water goes from this pump to each side of the cutting blade. This water keeps the dust down and the blade cool. Diamond blades will get hot, lose their temper, warp and become worthless in a very short time if not kept cool.

This saw is built for straight cuts. Frames and templates will have to be built if other cuttings are needed, or the stone will have to be tipped by hand and held for the desired proper cutting.

TOOLS FOR POLISHING, SMOOTHING AND SPLITTING STONE

There are various powered tools. Some have various size heads for wroughting and polishing stone (Fig. 1-19).

Fig. 1-18. A motor-powered stone saw makes clean cuts when splitting stone.

Fig. 1-19. (A) is a polishing head. (B) is a toothed chisel. (C) is a chisel and bolster. (D) is a punch or pointed chisel. (E) is a bush hammer tool. (F) is a sander and polisher.

Figure 1-19A is a polishing head. A toothed chisel or bolster type is used for dressing stones down to smooth faces and for cleaning and finishing moldings (Fig. 1-19B). Figure 1-19C is also used as a chisel and bolster. A punch or pointed chisel is ideal for sinking holes and removing superficial waste (Fig. 1-19D). A bush hammer tool can produce fine finishes on stone (Fig. 1-19E). Figure 1-19F is a sander and polisher used as a rubbing stone.

Some of these tools have handles or shanks which fit power drills and others are operated by a hammer-drill. The shank bits are of different sizes as well as the working heads. Power drills and hammer drills are also made in various sizes and stengths (horse-power).

Hand Rubbing Stones

The hand rubbing stones with a silicone carbide aggregate are fast cutting. They can be used to advantage when a powered rubbing stone cannot be used. Any of the hard granite stones with a true flat surface will cut softer stone when used (Fig. 1-20).

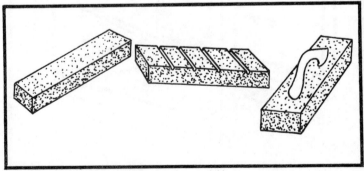

Fig. 1-20. Hand rubbing stones cut stone quickly.

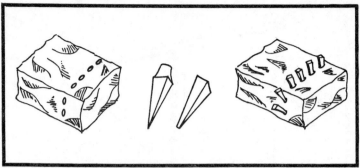

Fig. 1-21. These feather wedges help to break or split stone.

Feather Wedges

Feather wedges are used in breaking or splitting stone. First the stones are drilled a few inches apart and the feathers inserted. Then they are tapped in consecutive order until the stones are split (Fig. 1-21).

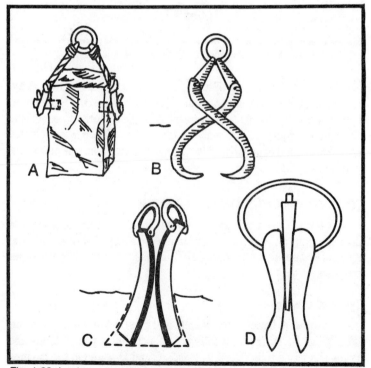

Fig. 1-22. Lewises are used for lifting and moving stone. (A) is inserted into stone. (B) acts like tongs and grabs the stone. (C) and (D) fasten in cavities.

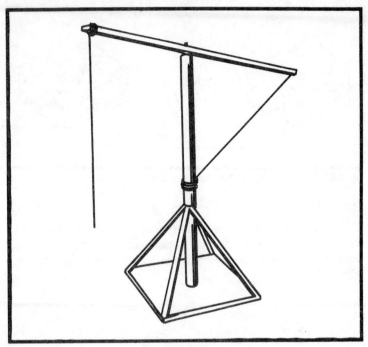

Fig. 1-23. A derrick is helpful when lifting big stones.

Feathers are made in different sizes, widths and lengths. They should be placed all around a stone where it is to be cut. Expensive, larger stone or fabricated stone require this method, especially when power tools are not available for cutting. There is less chance of ruining a good expensive or hard-to-get stone when this method of cutting is used.

TOOLS FOR SECURING AND LIFTING STONE

A *lewis* is used to secure a stone. Insert part of the lewis in a hole in a stone and use it to lift and move the stone. There are several kinds of lewises that can be made or purchased and used for the same purpose.

Types of Lewises

Lewis A is fastened to dowels and inserted in the stone to be lifted (Fig. 1-22). Lewis B in Fig. 1-22 acts like a pair of tongs and grabs the stone to be lifted. Lewises C and D fasten in the cavities made for the purpose of holding them when the stone is lifted (Fig. 1-22).

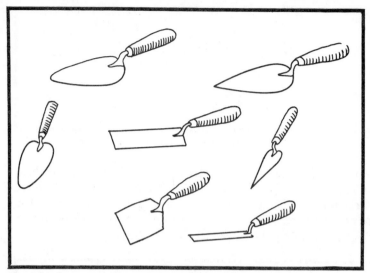

Fig. 1-24. Stone workers could not get along without trowels.

Derricks

The *derrick* is used for lifting large stones for the stonemason to work or set. One kind of derrick used by the stonemason is in Fig. 1-23. There are different kinds of derricks and lifting machines, and some are motor-powered. A powered crane is also used when setting large stone.

TROWELS

Trowels, are of various kinds and sizes. They have their special uses in stonework by the stonemason (Fig. 1-24). I like the wide-heel trowel which, I believe, is more adapted to placing the mortar when doing cobble or rubble stonework (Fig. 1-25). The narrow heeled trowel, is sometimes best for handling mortar when doing ashlar stonework (Fig. 1-26). The trowel in Fig. 1-27 comes in handy

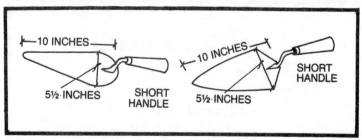

Fig. 1-25. A wide-heel trowel is a must when doing cobble or rubble stonework.

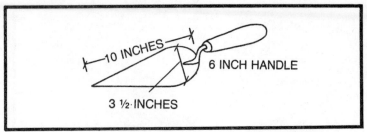

Fig. 1-26. A narrow-heel trowel is fine when doing ashlar stonework.

when filling joints. A small trowel is effective for joint work on cobble or rubble stonework (Fig. 1-28). Figure 1-29 is used for filling and slicking joints. The trowel shown in Fig. 1-30 is used for bucket mixing of mortar. Hawks come in many sizes and are ideal for holding mortar when filling joints or tucking (Fig. 1-31).

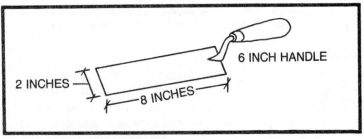

Fig. 1-27. This trowel fills joints well.

MEASURING AND MARKING DEVICES

The *rule* is used for measuring distances from points to points and angular markings. It also acts as a wall guide for elevations. The rule is marked off in feet, inches and fractions of an inch (Fig. 1-32). A rule (bricklayer's rule) has elevation markings which are handy when setting stone in courses.

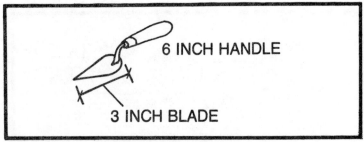

Fig. 1-28. This small trowel is handy for joint work.

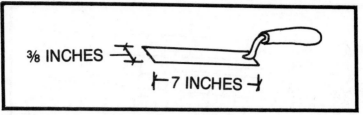

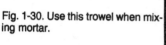

Fig. 1-29 A trowel for slicking joints.

Tape Rules

There are also tape rules. Some of these metal or plastic tape rules are self-winding and will automatically rewind themselves back into their boxes after use. Some tapes can be locked and stay unwound until the catch is released, thereby letting them rewind.

Fig. 1-30. Use this trowel when mixing mortar.

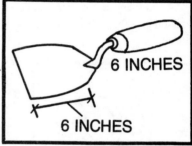

Measuring Tape and Chalk Box

The measuring tape is used for measuring distances from point to point. The tape is marked off as is the rule. It can be procured in various lengths (Fig. 1-33).

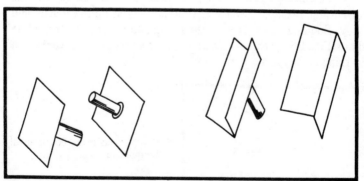

Fig. 1-31. The hawk comes in many sizes. It holds mortar while joints are filled.

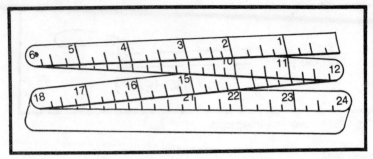

Fig. 1-32. A rule is essential when making measurements.

The chalk box makes line markings. The box contains a line and colored powders are put in the box. The line covered with color is snapped when stretched from point to point. It leaves a good clear marking when needed on stonework (Fig. 1-34).

A chalk line or any line can be chalked by a colored chalk-cake and used just like a chalk box line. This chalk-cake comes in different colors.

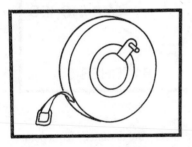

Fig. 1-33. Measuring tape is marked off like a rule.

Framing and Combination and Bevel Squares

The *framing square* is used for measuring and marking material for cutting, sizing and shaping. It is marked off on the tongue and body. Some squares have tables and quantity scales imprinted on them (Fig. 1-35). The *combination and bevel squares* are used when marking angles and for measuring (Fig. 1-36).

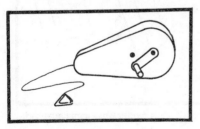

Fig. 1-34. The chalk box is ideal when marking lines.

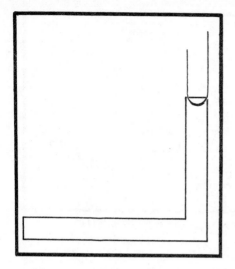

Fig. 1-35. A framing square is another measuring tool.

Plumb Bob

The *plumb bob* is used during plumbing masonry in order to keep stone setting work perpendicular. The line has various weight bobs suspended from it. In windy weather, the line should be protected from the wind to insure accurate plumbing (Fig. 1-37).

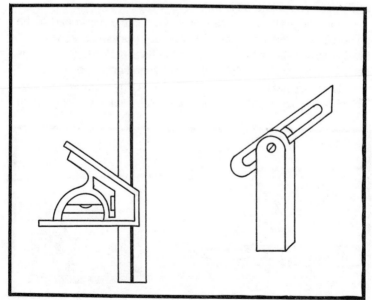

Fig. 1-36. The combination and bevel square is used when marking angles.

Fig. 1-37. The plumb line keeps stone setting work perpendicular.

Levels

The *levels* are used for plumbing and leveling during stonework construction. They are of various lengths (Fig. 1-38).

Some levels have only one vial. There are marks on the vial. When the bubble is between these marks, the level will be horizontal, or that area on which the level rests will be horizontal. True horizontal position can be found by switching the ends of the level on which it rests. If the bubble is in the previous exact position, the level and whatever it rests on is horizontally true.

Some levels have vials at each end and in the center part of the level. Other levels have two vials in these places. These types of levels can be read with any edge of the level next to that which is being leveled or checked, whether horizontal or perpendicular.

There are also small levels that hook on a tight line for leveling. There is the hand glass level scope used by some masons. Then

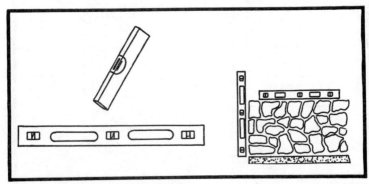

Fig. 1-38. Levels come in many lengths.

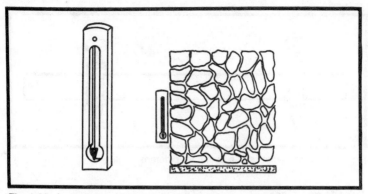

Fig. 1-39. A plumb line level is being replaced by vial levels.

there is the transit level used by masons as well as surveyors. There is a hose or flexible plastic or rubber tube level. This level contains water or some other liquid. It has a glass tube on its end. The hose is set or held at a mark (benchmark) or wherever desired. Since liquid seeks the same level, the tube end can be held up or down to where the liquid at the mark end is at the same elevation as the liquid at the glass end. The liquid at the glass end will be at the same elevation as that at the tube end. This method will locate the horizontal alignment of the two ends.

Plumb Bob Line

The plumb bob line level is used as a plumb level. It has given way to the more handy vial levels (Fig. 1-39).

Compasses

The *compass* is used for layout work (Fig. 1-40). The rod compass can be set for various lengths which is handy on job layout work. The rod compass can have a marking lead or a pencil inserted in one of its points for markings (Fig. 1-41).

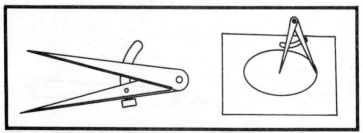

Fig. 1-40. This standard compass is used for layout work.

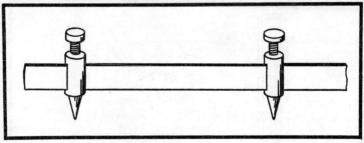

Fig. 1-41. A rod compass can be set for different lengths.

Pencils and Lines

Pencils and marking tools are needed on all stonework construction for the purpose of marking for exactness when needed (Fig. 1-42).

There are various kinds of marking pencils. The lead pencil has different hardnesses of lead and many different colors. There is a soapstone pencil for marking on metal. A nail or sharp metal and the trowel point are also used for marking on stone.

One of the best marks to use, rather than a straight mark, check-or-cross, is just a dot that is circled. It can be seen from 15 to 20 feet away and is an exact point mark.

A mason's line is used as a wall guide when setting stone. A nylon line will stretch with less sag than do lines made with other material (Fig. 1-43).

Pins and Line Blocks

Pins and line blocks are used to hold the mason's line when a line is used (Fig. 1-44). The line holding blocks shown are made of wood or metal. There are various shaped line blocks. Their use is fine if they can be held where put.

Fig. 1-42. Use pencils for marking on stone.

Fig. 1-43. This mason's line aids you when setting stone.

The line or a nail is also used to hold lines. A wide pin is best. It will hold a line from slipping better than does a nail. Also shown is the line twig clip (Fig. 1-44).

CUTTER, TWIGS, RUBBING STONES AND HEATERS

Cutters are used for snipping wire and small reinforcing rods (Fig. 1-45). Cutters are of several kinds. All of them will cut wire. Some cutters will cut small bars and pencil steel. The bolt cutter is used for cutting larger reinforcing rods and bolts (Fig. 1-46). Again, this tool comes in different sizes. The smaller bolt cutters are handy when it comes to cutting pencil steel and heavy ties that tin snips cannot cut.

The *twig* is used between the points of a stretched mason's line for the purpose of keeping the line in alignment as well as preventing

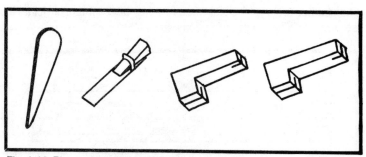

Fig. 1-44. Pins and line blocks hold the mason's line.

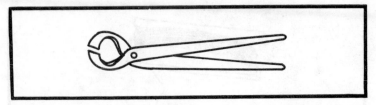

Fig. 1-45. A wire cutter is a handy tool.

it from sagging (Fig. 1-47). There are times that more than one twig is used, especially when it is windy. These twigs will maintain straighter line against the wind. A straight line will keep a batter out of a stone wall.

Rubbing stones smooth stones down to a much finer surface. They are operated either by hand or power (Fig. 1-48).

The round metal disk turns under the stone. Sand is put in the box as pictured to a depth of about ½-inch to 2 inches above the disk. This sharp sand and metal filings help grind to its face finish.

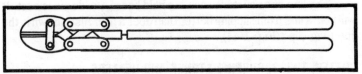

Fig. 1-46. Bolt cutters can snip heavy duty material.

Heaters are of various kinds: gas, electric and fuel (Fig. 1-49). They are operated when the temperature may cause freezing. A metal oil barrel homemade stove is also used. Wood or coal can be burned in it. A frame covered with canvas or plastic will keep the heat where it is needed. Heat should not dry out the mortar before it is set.

JOINTER TOOLS

Jointer tools are helpful when forming different mortar joints in stonework. They come in various sizes.

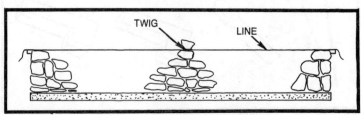

Fig. 1-47. A twig prevents a mason's line from sagging.

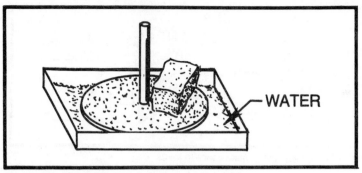

Fig. 1-48. Rubbing stones can work by hand or power.

Jointers are made of steel, copper, glass and plastic. Temporary jointers can be made of wood. The trowel handle has been used as a jointer. Some joints are brushed out with a steel or stiff bristle brush and called finished (Fig. 1-50). Figures 1-51 through 1-60 show different jointers and a scutch.

BRUSHES, PAILS, TUB AND MORTAR TABLE

Brushes are obviously used for brushing in stonework.

The brush in Fig. 1-61 is a stonemason's cleaning brush. It is handy to brush loose mortar from the joints just before they take their semi-set.

This brush should not be used too soon before the joint mortar is semi-set, or the joint will show the brush marks. However, when the brushing is done before the setting starts, the joints should be restruck with the jointer. Too early brushing will mess up the stonework with mortar.

Fig. 1-49. Heaters are welcome devices during winter months.

Fig. 1-50. These jointers make concave joints.

Figure 1-62 is a whisk broom that is used to sweep particles and sometimes mortar from mortar joints and brickwork. This brush can also rake out semi-set joints on stonework. The brush is held flat to the joint with pressure when used as a jointer.

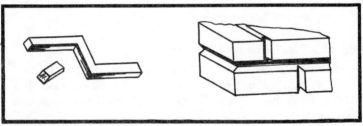

Fig. 1-51. This jointer makes V-joints.

Figure 1-63 is a wire brush with a scraper on its end. It is used where stubborn set mortar needs to be cleaned off stonework.

On some stone that does not contain too large a quantity of iron, an acid wash is used when cleaning stonework after it is fully set. This wash will loosen the mortar, which is easier to clean off with this wire brush. The stonework should be thoroughly washed down with water before and after this wash and cleaning is done.

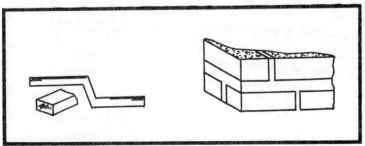

Fig. 1-52. Use this jointer for flat joints.

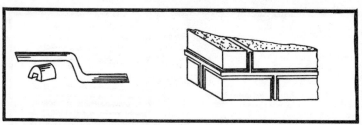

Fig. 1-53. Projected joints are made with this jointer.

The acid solution is prepared as follows: Mix 10 percent to 15 percent muriatic acid to 100 percent water. This solution will not harm concrete. It will eat paint and varnish. The acid brings out the mineral in stone and makes stonework look old if it is not washed off

Fig. 1-54. This jointer makes projected and convex joints.

after use. The brush should be rinsed with water or the acid solution will eat the brush metal bristles. It is necessary to wear plastic or rubber gloves when washing brushes. The acid is harmful to your hands.

Fig. 1-55. Make groove-like joints with this jointer.

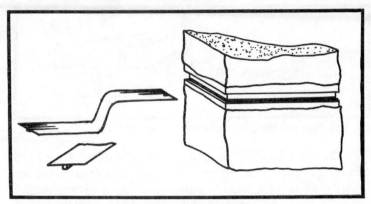

Fig. 1-56. This jointer makes square, recessed joints.

The brush in Fig. 1-64 is handy to use as a water throwing brush when mortar is put into dry joints. Known as a splash brush, it has thick, long bristles and should not be used in an acid wash. A tampico fiber brush is not readily eaten up by an acid or masonry wash (Fig. 1-65). All brushes should be washed and cleaned after use. The brushes in Fig. 1-66 are scrub brushes and are used when washing down stonework.

Pails are made of rubber, plastic and baked clay (Fig. 1-67). They may be lined with porcelain enamel. Acid will not "eat" these kinds of pails. Use acid when washing down stonework which will not rust. Nevertheless, strong lye soap is safer to use.

A tub is handy when mixing small batches or joint mortars (Fig. 1-68).

A mortar table is a necessity when doing stonework. It holds the mortar for the stone mason (Fig. 1-69).

Fig. 1-57. Flat joints are accomplished with this tool.

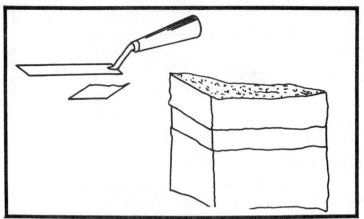

Fig. 1-58. This jointer can slick flat surfaces.

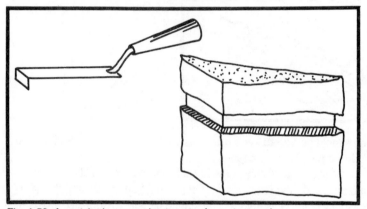

Fig. 1-59. A scutch cleans semi-set mortar from stonework.

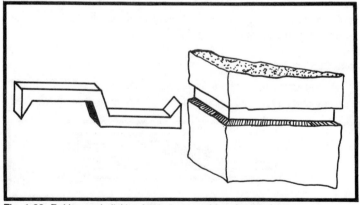

Fig. 1-60. Raking and slicking joints is no problem for this jointer.

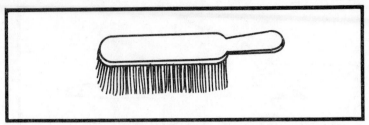

Fig. 1-61. A stonemason's cleaning brush sweeps loose mortar from joints.

SCAFFOLDS, TABLES AND BARRELS

There are many kinds of *scaffolds* (Fig. 1-70). Some types can be stacked one on the other to any height required. The stonemason's runway can be moved up as the work progresses. All scaffold-

Fig. 1-62. Whisk brooms sweep mortar from brickwork.

ing should be tied to keep progresses. All scaffolding should be tied to keep people from tripping.

Scaffolds generally come in parts and can be readily assembled and knocked down in a hurry. They should be strong and stable as masonry material is heavy. You should be able to adjust scaffolds to the different heights or lifts of stonework setting without having to take them down for reassembly. When a wood scaffold is used, it should be nailed well. Scaffolds should have ample room for the material and the workman (Fig. 1-70).

Stone Cutting Table

A stone cutting table is always nice to have (Fig. 1-71). It should be strong and have a semi-soft top that gives when stone is worked

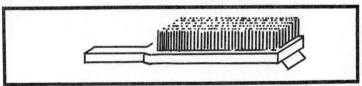

Fig. 1-63. A wire brush with a scraper is used to brush off tough mortar.

38

Fig. 1-64. Do not use a splash brush in an acid wash.

or wrought. A rubber top is best. Some stonemasons use a sand box in which to wrought stone. The stone cutting table will be taken up again in this book.

Fig. 1-65. A tampico fiber brush can be used in acid.

Wood and Metal Barrels

A *barrel* is ideal for holding water, lime, putty or whatever. The barrel can be made of wood or metal. A wood barrel will cake up in the inside and should be wetted down before use. The metal barrel, if made of steel or iron, will cake up and rust, thereby getting scales and rust in the lime putty. It should be well cleaned after use. A galvanized barrel or tub is a good one to use (Fig. 1-72).

Fig. 1-66. These scrub brushes wash down stonework.

39

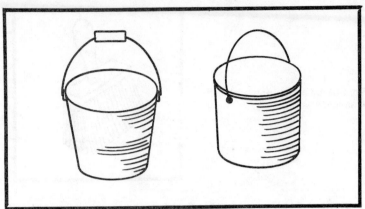

Fig. 1-67. Pails hold washing solutions.

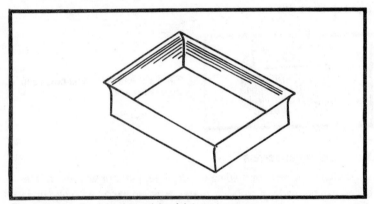

Fig. 1-68. Use the tub when mixing joint mortars.

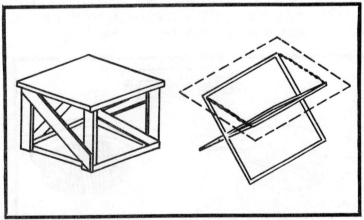

Fig. 1-69. Mortar tables are a must when doing masonry work.

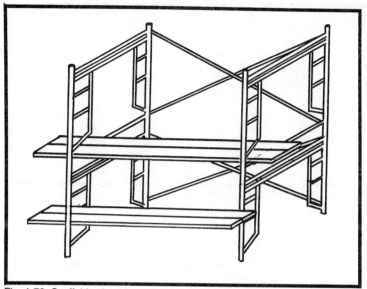
Fig. 1-70. Scaffolds should be strong to support heavy weights.

OTHER EQUIPMENT

A shovel is a very handy tool. A long-handled one with a flat, straight blade is best.

A hoe with holes in its blade and a long handle is used when mixing mortar by hand. The hoe can keep the mix from collecting at one end of the box when the box has a curvature at the end.

Shovels and hoes need cleaning, even during their use. This action will keep semi-set material out of the mortar. Unclean shovels and hoes left and stored with mortar on them will rust (Fig. 1-73).

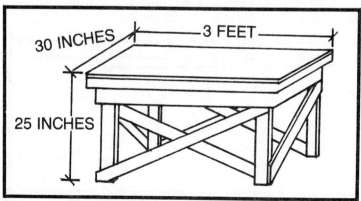
Fig. 1-71. A rubber top is best for a stone cutting table.

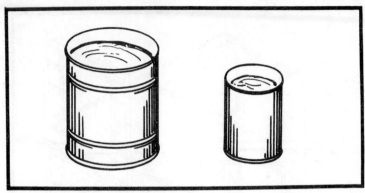

Fig. 1-72. Barrels are useful containers.

Mixing Box

A mixing box can be used for slacking lime or mixing mortar (Fig. 1-74). I like a box made of metal. They can be made in a size that is best fitted for their use.

A galvanized metal box is preferable to either a wooden one or a metal one that will rust. A box can be purchased or made. It should have straight sides and the ends should be slanted from the bottom.

Hod

A *hod* carries mortar or material to the stonemason (Fig. 1-75). A wheelbarrow, pail or two-wheel cart is also used (Fig. 1-76). The hod and all mortar-hauling equipment should be kept clean at all times from semi-set material.

Screens

The *screen* filters sand and other material. This screen can have either ⅛ or ¼-inch holes in it. The side and top end boards keep the

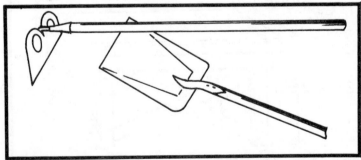

Fig. 1-73. Shovels and hoes are handy pieces of equipment.

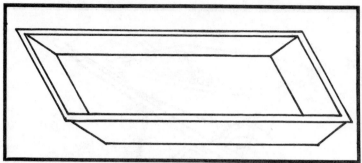

Fig. 1-74. Galvanized metal mixing boxes work best.

sand coming out as it is thrown in the screen for screening. If thrown in at the top, the sand has a longer chance to work through the screen than if it were thrown or scattered at the screen's bottom.

The screen can be adjusted by the braces to create a more or less degree of slant (incline). Wet sand takes longer to screen and requires less degree of incline than does dry sand (Fig. 1-77).

The screens in Fig. 1-78 are used when screening very fine material. Some of them are made with hair. A metal hardware cloth screen will last longer.

Finer sand is required when pitching and in many cases when tucking old stonework. Fine sand is required for mortar used when setting marble and fully wrought stone.

Measuring Box

A measuring box is a handy device to use when measuring material for accuracy (Fig. 1-79). It should hold 1 cubic foot of

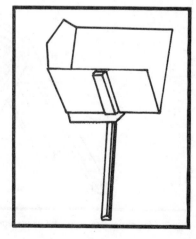

Fig. 1-75. A hod carries mortar and other material.

43

Fig. 1-76. A wheelbarrow performs the same function as a hod.

material. The box does not have a bottom. It is placed in the mixing box, filled and then lifted up, off and out of the mixing box.

When measuring sand, an allowance will have to be made if the sand is damp, moist or saturated with water. Sand can bulk up to as much as 25 percent of its dry size when wet.

Snips

The *snips* cut flashing during the course of stonework construction, which includes chimney and foundation flashing. There are various kinds of snips. The straight cutting ones are generally used

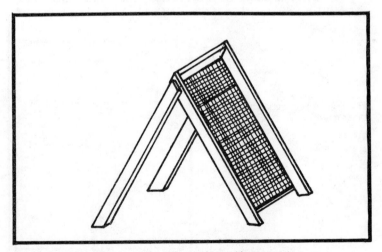

Fig. 1-77. This screen is useful when working with aggregate.

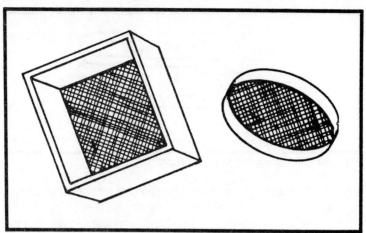

Fig. 1-78. Metal hardware cloth screens last the longest.

(Fig. 1-80). But the kind in Fig. 1-81 will cut out round circles better. They will also do straight cutting.

Caulking Guns

A caulking gun, is used when caulking around windows and door frames to keep out moisture. It is also used as a tucking tool when putting mortar in joints (Fig. 1-82).

The mortar gun is much larger than the caulking gun. These guns are rust-resistent and will hold from ½ to 3 quarts of caulking and grouting mortar or other material. The grip trigger has to be

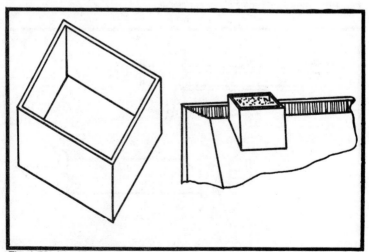

Fig. 1-79. A measuring box does not have a bottom.

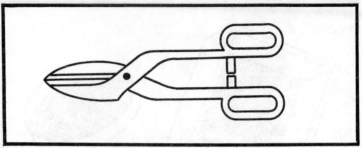

Fig. 1-80. A straight-cutting pair of tin snips.

squeezed to make it work. There are different size spouts that can be used.

Power Mixers

A power mixer is used for mixing mortar. There are various sizes, kinds and makes. Mixers are powered by fuel, electricity and by hand.

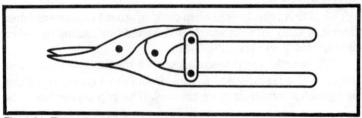

Fig. 1-81. These tin snips can cut out circles.

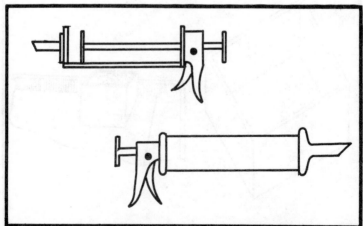

Fig. 1-82. Caulking guns hold up to 3 quarts of caulking material.

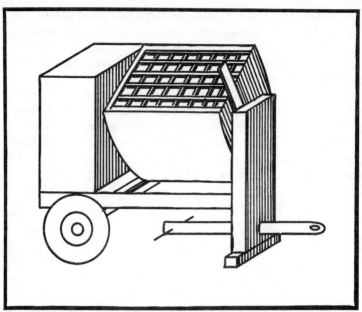

Fig. 1-83. This mixer is best for making mortar.

Fig. 1-84. This mixer is ideal for mixing cement.

The mixer in Fig. 1-83 is the best type for making mortar. The mixer in Fig. 1-84 is also good, and it is the best type to use when mixing cement. All mixers should be kept clean and free from scale and semi-set material. These mixers will combine the materials together before water is added.

The mixer in Fig. 1-84 works best if some water is put in it at the start. Gravel is put in next. The sand is put·in and then the binder is added. If water is not added, there will be no mixing action.

The mixer in Fig. 1-83 will work best for mixing dry material first. The cross pedals do a good job of moving the dry mix before water is added. Color is always added to the binder if color is used.

Chapter 2
Stone Classifications

The evolutionary processes in the earth's manufacture diversifies stone, changes its structural arrangement and varies its constituent components. The following explanation of stone is necessary in order to choose, handle, work and build with stone.

Building or structural stone originates from igneous, metamorphic, and sedimentary rock. A piece broken from rock is a stone. Granite, slate, sandstone and limestone are durable construction stones. Each has a durability according to the proportion of its component elements and physical structure; each has a strength governed by its compactness; and each has its own appearance and beauty, governed to a great extent by the iron oxide present. Rocks are variously classified, depending on the geologist classifying them. Decomposed primary rock (clastics) start a new generation by being part of a new rock, secondary rock (sedimentary rock). Sedimentary rock are clastic, stratified and generally fossiliferous sandstone, conglomerates, shales, etc. Also, there are the limestones, containing fossil remains. Marbles and dolomites are varieties of limestone. Igneous rocks formed from plutonic materials, once in a molten condition, are effusive rock (lava-like), intrusive rock (magna forced into veins and fissures, etc.) and plutonic rock (granites and others formed by great pressure at the deepest depth and coming to a crystalline state). Between the sedimentary (secondary) rock class and igneous (primary) rock is a class of rocks called metamorphic rock. These rocks have been produced from both primary and secondary rocks by enormous heat and pressure. They have been crystallized. This recrystallization changes limestone into marble.

These stones make good building stone. They vary in hardness even within their classifications. When wroughting the hard brittle ones, care should be taken. The stone may split apart and be ruined.

The softer stone works much easier. Care is necessary, especially when there is a fracture, vein or fault in the stone. The stone may come apart and become smaller than the desired size.

The tools used to wrought granite will require a hammer if hand work is performed. The sets, chisels, punches, points and picks should be at least of two-point carbon steel and be kept sharp. The size of the hammer to use will depend on the hardness and size of stone. The size of tools used will depend on the granite stone to be wrought.

The degree that a tool is set to a stone will generally chip, scale or split a stone in the direction of force. Practice will show the degree of pitch a tool should have when wroughting stone. Granite can and is sawed by powered saws.

GRANITE

Granite is classed as metamorphic or igneous rock, depending on the geologist. It has dominant crystalline components (feldspar, mica, hornblende, and quartz, along with magnetite and iron, which give different effects of appearance), and is one of the best building stones. When stratified, it can be easily split along its cleavage plane. When not stratified, stout pitching tools are required to shape it into a usable building stone.

Granite is textured from fine to coarse-grained. It has shades of grays, reds, greens and yellows. Its weight varies in different localities, which is from 160 to 172 pounds per cubic foot (Fig. 2-1).

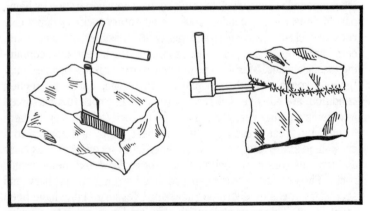

Fig. 2-1. Granite is an excellent stone for construction work.

Fig. 2-2. A wide chisel is used to split sandstone.

SANDSTONE

Sandstone is a sedimentary rock formed by the cementation of grains of sand by silica, calcium sulfate, clays, calcium carbonate and iron oxide, which gives sandstone its color. The best building sandstone has a siliceous cement binder.

Sandstone taken from thick rock beds can be worked and split in any direction. It does not have to be set horizontally along its natural bed plane, as does thin-bedded sandstone, to maintain its greatest strength and withstand pressure without crushing or cracking. The weight of sandstone varies in different localities, with a difference in weight from 140 to 144 pounds per cubic foot.

The stone set and hammer are used when wroughting sandstone. A wide sharp chisel is also employed when spliting sandstone (Fig. 2-2). The set and hammer are generally used in forming the arris of sandstone. Where there is a cleavage plane in the sandstone being wrought, care must be taken. The sandstone may split along its cleavage plane and ruin the stones for size.

The harder and finer the texture of sandstone, the easier it is to wrought as required. Course textured sandstone will in many cases slough off when worked, especially when forming the arris. Sandstone can be easily sawed by a power saw. Either wet or dry saw blades may be used.

LIMESTONE

Limestone is a sedimentary rock consisting largely of calcium carbonate. It may contain silica, clay, aluminum, magnesium, iron

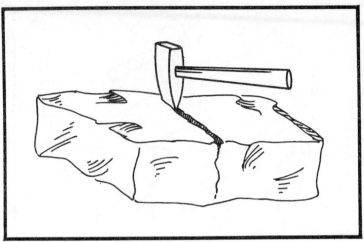

Fig. 2-3. Limestone has many uses in stonework.

oxide and other carbonaceous material in varying quantities. Impurities in limestone give it a variety of colors such as grays, blacks, browns and reds, in different depths of color. Its texture is from fine to coarse.

Most limestone can be used for building purposes. However, there are limestones that are subject to efflorescence and are not as good for stonework as the dolomite limestones (calcium carbonate and magnesium). Freestone limestone from thick beds, and free of cleavage plane has equal strength in all directions, and can be worked without cracking where not wanted. It will not fracture except in the line of force of the pitching tools or hammer. It can be set in any direction and act as floor tile, plinths, steps and grade courses. Freestone limestone will withstand abrasion and wear. The weight of limestone is from 170 to 184 pounds per cubic foot.

Limestone is a pretty stone. If it is selected with care, it can make a blend of colorful stonework. A mottled appearance is easily made by choice of various colors and color depths. This stone is wrought by hand tools or by a power saw and power tools (Fig. 2-3).

MARBLE

Marble is a metamorphic rock composed of calcium carbonate, dolomite or both. It is generally recrystallized limestone, and formed, usually, in regions of metamorphic rocks. It differs greatly in color, from black to white, and varies in hardness and texture. It will be difficult to polish when chlorite and scales of mica are present;

however, they add to the beauty and attractiveness of marble. White marble is pure marble.

Serpentine marbles run from yellows to reds, browns and greens and have a glassy luster. They are often matted or spotted.

Marble can be handled and wrought as other stones. But care should be taken to select marble that is of the same hardness and color in order to maintain as near a uniform appearance and quality of durability as possible throughout the building's life.

Travertine has been used in construction for centuries. Large deposits are quarried in Italy, and plentiful amounts of this rock are found in and near Yellowstone Park in the United States. It is handled and worked in much the same way as marble. Travertine appears worm-eaten, unless its texture is of a coherently nonporous consolidated mass.

The weight of marble varies depending on the locality. It will weigh from 168 to 174 pounds per cubic foot (Fig. 2-4).

SLATE

Slate is a fine-grained metamorphic rock, formed of low-grade regional metamorphism of shale. Slate rock contains quartz, calcite, dolomite, sericite, chlorite, graphite, mica, hematite and iron sulfide. Slate can be split into very thin, small and large sheets. It is used as floor tile, roof tile, stair tread, risers, wainscot, trim and veneer. It can be honed to a dull polish. Slates are in many shades of

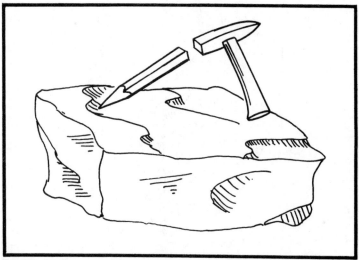

Fig. 2-4. Marble, particularly travertine, has been used in construction for many years.

reds, greens, grays and blacks. Some slate, called "fading slate," will not keep its color when exposed to air.

Slate is a very durable stone, and will not break easily except along its laminations (cleavage planes). Holes can be punched through its sheets quite easily with a punch. Its weight is fairly light. However, some slate rocks weigh as much as 166 pounds per cubic foot.

Slate is generally sawed to size, after it is split into sheets. Slate is a tough stone and is tough to cut to size after it is parted into sheets. With practice slate can be sized with hand tools (Fig. 2-5).

OTHER CONSTRUCTION STONES

There are other construction stones which should be briefly discussed. For instance, one is the oil stone shale which may not be

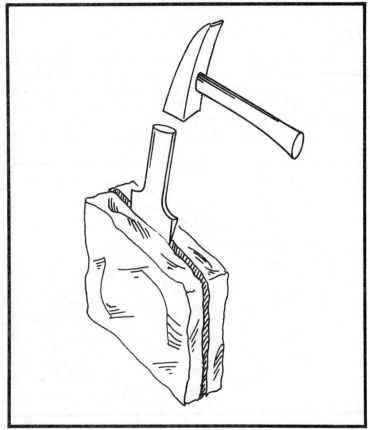

Fig. 2-5. Slate will not break easily.

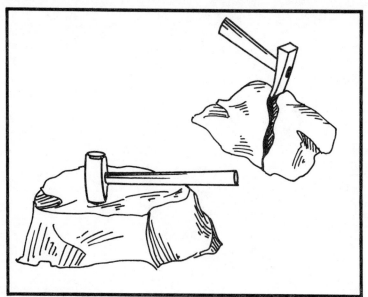
Fig. 2-6. These stones are used in cobweb stonework.

wise to use when a fireplace is built. Fieldstone, which is somewhat rounded, is used in cobblestone work and called cobblestone. When this stone is split, pitched, and set with its fresh face out, it gives the effect and appearance of cobwebs and makes what is called cobweb stonework. This stonework will not sustain a heavy load. It is best used in garden walks or curtain walls and veneer stonework. The weight of this stone varies greatly, averaging approximately 158 pounds per cubic foot (Fig. 2-6).

Chapter 3
Artificial Stone

Artificial stone should resemble the natural stone it is intended to simulate. It should be pressured from its top down in its making, and should be set in stonework with its top up. Every 2 inches of the poured mix should be well-tamped. This tamping pressures the artificial stone in its making. A well-pressured artificial stone will sustain more load without cracking or crushing under load pressure than will an untamped artificial stone. The texture and color of artificial stone would also resemble the natural stone it is supposed to represent.

Artificial stone can be wrought as are natural stones. This stone works best when wroughting if it is fully cured (Fig. 3-1).

ARTIFICIAL STONE MIXES

A *binder* is used when making a stone mix. Cements and limes are the best binders to use. Hydrated lime, stain and waterproof cements and their combinations are ideal binders for they will withstand the outside elements best. Other binders may be used, such as common cements and limes, where the artificial stone is protected and not subject to pressure, extreme temperature changes, moisture, etc. Good binders and aggregates, along with clean water, make the best and longest lasting artificial stone.

AGGREGATES

When you are fabricating artificial stone, a graded aggregate of sand or finely crushed stone will produce a texture similar to natural stone. Natural aggregates are best to use as they will withstand the elements with which the finished stone will come in contact. However, artificial aggregates are also utilized.

Artificial aggregate chips can be made either with or without an aggregate. The binder should be (but not neccessary) white stain and waterproof cement. Very fine aggregate should be used where aggregate is employed. Color (mineral color) as required should be in the mix. Water which is drinkable and free of sulfur and salt, is necessary to start the mixing action. The proportion of binder to aggregate (including color) should never be more than 50 percent aggregate. When the artificial stone is to be polished, the aggregate is not used. The water should be added sparingly and thoroughly mixed until the mix is evenly wet and stiff. The mix should not be so stiff that it cannot be rolled or spread out on a well-oiled platform to a depth of ⅛ to ⅜ inches thick. When nearly set (semi-set), it should be cut into irregular pieces or particles. The mix should be kept from drying out until it is set hard. Various colored chips should be made that are near the color of the particles in the natural stone. Small trial mixes will prove worthwhile in determining the amount of color to use. White chips are made without color. The aggregate in the mix should be either white sand or white chips. Or you can use no aggregate.

The color used should be the best fade-resistant kind, preferably a mineral color. Color should be used sparingly, as too much color weakens a mix. Colors can be mixed or blended together for some shades. It is best to mix the color with the binder before the binder is put in the mix. Water used should be free from impurities such as sulfur, alkali, salt, etc.

ARTIFICIAL STONE MAKING

There are many mix formulas for making artificial stone. Many formulas with specific methods and equipment are patented; however, in this book all formulas and methods considered have been used by me and are not, to my knowledge, patented. There are also many patented products on the market that can be used when making artificial stone.

Binder and aggregate proportions, including color and water, can be varied to comply with local conditions (temperature, humidity, atmospheric pressure, etc.) and obtainable material in order to make artificial stone that will almost equal natural stone in strength and durability. Adhesive strength of a mix that has good cement as a binder increases more rapidly than does cohesive strength. Compressive strength of a mix that has good cement as a binder is, when cured, several times that of its tensile strength. Cement is un-

Fig. 3-1. Take care when working on the faces of these inserts.

equaled as a binder in a mix when durability and strength are required in an artificial stone. This should be kept in mind when proportioning a mix, and one must not use too small an amount of binder. In a mix it is absolutely essential that each particle of the aggregate is completely covered with the binder used. It is also imperative that every part of a mix is dampened enough with good clean water to create the chemical action necessary to change the well-blended mix into hard, durable artificial stone. Never use too much water. A good, dampened mix makes the best artificial stone. Experimentation with mixes of different proportions will prove worthwhile as well as interesting.

When an aggregate is used, you should have the mix as free from excess moisture as is possible. Too much water will wash the aggregate free from the binder and separation will result. Too much moisture will also cause the color to run.

Fine to very fine-graded aggregates are used when making artificial stone. Yet, some natural stones have various sizes of aggregate in them, and in some natural stone, these coarser aggregates and even chip can be used in a mix to represent natural stones. Voids should not be in artificial stone. Therefore, a graded aggregate should be used. In some natural stone the naked eye cannot distinguish the aggregate from the crystallized texture; in this case, very fine aggregate is sparingly used or not used. Some natural stone can be polished. When duplicating this stone, an artificial aggregate may be used. Then the artificial stone can be planed and polished. A wool rag will do a good job of polishing when a power polisher is not available.

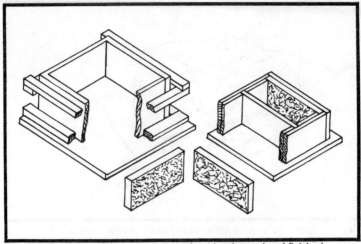

Fig. 3-2. The faces of these stones need not be dressed and finished.

Various mixes can be used in duplicating natural stones. The face can be of several different colors, blends, mottled textures—even stratified. The stratas may be of different shades and colors as well as textures. In stone casting, the body-back can be of different material mixes than the faces; color is not needed for the backing as it will not show in stonework, unless it is a quoin where two faces are necessary.

For outside artificial stone that is white, mottled or stratified, a white cement is best. A white or light-colored sand should then be used. Portland cement can be used for colored stone. For inside use, an artificial stone, whether colored or not, may have its binder of Keen cement if desired.

Cast stone should be kept from drying out until it is fully hard. It should be kept from freezing. The stone can be covered with wet sand, sawdust, straw, sacking, etc., and kept damp for approximately eight to 11 days.

The face of artificial stone can be as follows.

■ **Mix one.** Use one part cement to ¼ part very fine sand or powdered stone. The color desired can be added. Use water sparingly. Pound this mix against the form face.

■ **Mix two.** Stir one part cement to one part aggregate (graded as required). Add color and water. Mix stiff and ram into form face.

■ **Mix three.** Use one part cement and ¼ part hydrated lime to 1½ parts aggregate of your choice. Add color, water and mix well. Have the mix stiff and ram into form face.

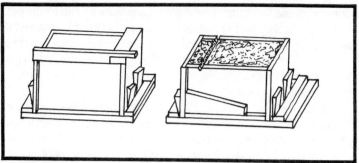

Fig. 3-3. You can buy or rent many forms and inserts.

■ **Mix four.** Use one part portland cement to three parts graded aggregate (fine and coarse). Add water for a very stiff mix and ram the mix into the form against face mixes one, two or three. Cover the mix and keep it damp until it has fully set hard, approximately 11 days. These mixes will make strong, durable artificial stone.

Artificial stone is made in factories that are equipped with patented machines, using patented forms, molds and dies. The equipment is adjustable and can turn out various sizes of fabricated stone. Such methods employ pressure and vibratory compaction. Curing rooms, heat, spray and steam are used in these plants. Plant chemists and engineers continually test all component materials as well as the finished product. The artificial stones are sorted, culled and selected to meet desired standards before they are marketed.

Artificial stone is still made by hand in many parts of the world. Forms can be shaped to represent natural stone. Mold inserts are

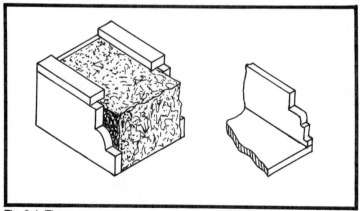

Fig. 3-4. These are more examples of artificial stone forms.

employed in the forms for the different face shapes. The forms can be of wood, metal, cast materials (plaster of Paris) or any material that will keep its shape. Shape and size of the finished stone governs the material and construction of the forms. Various patented forms and inserts may be purchased or rented (Figs. 3-3 and 3-4). Shellacked forms will not stick to the stone.

The face of the inserts in Fig. 3-2 is important. The face of the artificial stone need not be finished, dressed face. When cured it can be shaped, pitched and dressed, just as a quarried or natural stone can be wrought by hand or machine. But time and labor costs can be reduced if the stone is cast in a finished state.

Chapter 4
Building Stone

Building stone should be durable and able to withstand the elements. It must suit the purpose for which it is required.

Stone can be cut, shaped, carved and dressed in mills, shops, in quarries and on the job. This work of wroughting stone can be done with hand, pneumatic and electric tools. Or you can work with power tools at supply mills or on the job. Rough quarried and wrought stone can be purchased in almost every part of the world.

The buying and selling of stone varies in different localities, with respect to quantity, quality and price. Quantity is by measure or by weight (ton). If the perch (by size) is 16½ cubic feet and the weight is 2000 pounds, the price still varies if sold by the yard (27 cubic feet) or cord (4 feet wide, 4 feet high, and 8 feet long). The price also differs according to the kind, quality and size of stone requested. Some stones are not local, and a stone dealer will have shipping and handling charges to add to the price.

CUTTING BUILDING STONE

A powered saw along with powered stone tools are not a must, but are nice to have when building with stone. When cutting or wroughting stone, it is necessary to be very careful as the work progresses (Fig. 4-1). A finishing blow with a hammer has more than once ruined a stone. There is generally a place in stonework for almost any size stone. The stone's length, in proportion to its breadth and depth, may vary according to resistance to cracking when set in stonework. A good rule to follow on most kinds of

Fig. 4-1. Take great pains when cutting or wroughting stone.

building stone to be set in a load-bearing wall is to cut a stone no longer in length than five times its depth, or with its breadth less 1½ times its depth. This rule need not be followed in many trim and veneer jobs as they are not load-bearing.

I find it generally best to break some unworked stone into two or more units using the ax hammer or spalling hammer. A broad, heavy chisel and hammer is also utilized. Cut a draft (groove) and use the chisel-edged hammer. On heavy, wide slabs, each hit with the hammer will deepen the draft a little until the stone cracks along the draft. It may be necessary to give the stone a solid blow with the hammer on its backside opposite the draft before it will crack apart (Fig. 4-2).

Fig. 4-2. You may have to strike stubborn stones with a chisel-edged hammer to crack them.

64

Fig. 4-3. Feather wedges will be needed on some stones.

Some stone will require borings and possibly feathers to crack it apart (Fig. 4-3). Stratified stone is easily cut with hand tools.

When pitching the arris on fieldstone, a beveled set is the proper tool to use. The right size hammer for the tool and stone should be selected to prevent extra work.

Fieldstones (stone gathered from fields) can be split by hitting them with a heavy-weight hammer. They can also be used in cobblestone work. A split fieldstone can be pitched along its arris and set in cobweb stonework.

There will always be a need for hand tools when doing stonework. Machinery-finished stone, no matter how well done, will always require hand tool working before use in almost all kinds of stonework. The lengths of fully finished stone will have to be cut to fit the setting of stone (Fig. 4-4).

Fig. 4-4. Cut the lengths of finished stone.

Fig. 4-5. Semi-squared stone is used in rubble stonework.

Semi-squared or oblong stone can be used in rubble stonework. It is best to shape up the arris to conform to the face of the stonework (Fig. 4-5).

COPING STONE

Coping stone can be purchased or made in various shapes and sizes. This stone when properly wrought, whether rough or dressed, should have a moisture drip groove. Should the coping extend over on both sides, there should be an undercut groove on both underside edges. This groove wall helps keep water from running down the face of the stonework.

Coping should be sloped at its top for drainage. At the corner returns the coping should be sloped by winding where necessary (Fig. 4-6).

Stone can be shaped and carved to different pattern-like designs when needed. Figure 4-6 shows some of the many special purposes of wrought stone. The place and purpose of a stone in stonework determines its name (Fig. 4-7).

CLASSES OF STONE

There are four main classes of stone used in stonework: *rounded*, smooth-like stone (fieldstone), *rough quarry stone*, *accurately-squared dressed stone*, and *stratified stone*.

A rounded, smooth stone (stone of various sizes worn by the elements) is called *cobblestone*. It is used in cobble stone work. When it is split, it is utilized in cobweb stonework. It can also act as a veneer.

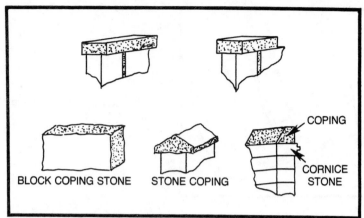

Fig. 4-6. Examples of coping stones.

An unsquared rough stone of various shapes and sizes is called *rubblestone*. It is used in rubble stonework. When its face is left rough in stonework, the stonework is called rustic rubble. Rubble stone can be pitched on an even arris.

Wrought dressed stone is shown in Chapter 1. However, machinery has, to a large extent, taken over the sizing, dressing and shaping of this kind of stone dressing. Powered hand tools are used for carving, edging, cutting, drilling, chipping, bush hammering, etc. Surfacing machines rough down stone to almost any finish. Grinding machines prepare a stone surface for polishing. Disc-cutting and

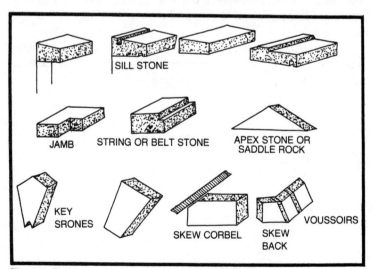

Fig. 4-7. These stones have different shapes and purposes.

Fig. 4-8. You can wind stone and make different shapes.

polishing lathes are also used to shape and finish stone. Sand-blasting renews the appearance of stonework.

Almost any wrought stone may be purchased. Rustic or split-face ashlar of different sizes and lengths can be purchased, including stones 2¼ inches or more in breadth which allows bonding with brick and other back-up units. Lengths of wrought stone vary from 1 to 5 foot lengths. When set in stonework, its face will protrude beyond the mortar joint making the rubble stonework neat with its finished appearance.

Accurately squared dressed stone is used in ashlar stonework. It can be dressed in the many face finishes of wrought stone.

Stratified stone can be used in rubble and ashlar stonework. It is often used as a veneer. When it is laid with its broad or top side as a face, it acts as a decorative veneer if thin, and if thick, as cobweb stonework.

Winding a stone to different shapes can be done by machinery or by hand. You can cut or sink running sinkings with a chisel and pick out the stone between the sinkings (Fig. 4-8).

Chapter 5
Dressed, Molded
and Scrolled Stone

The face of a stone can be dressed. If an end is also dressed, it can be a *quion*; if both ends are dressed, it can be a double quoin. A stone is considered rustic if its face is roughly wrought. If a rebate or groove is made along the top arris of the stone or the arris is chamfered, the stone is considered rusticated. If a stone is tooled to any of the standard dresses, it is considered fully wrought. A stone that is chiseled or tooled to a contour is considered a molded stone. A scroll stone is carved to a pattern -like design.

WROUGHT STONE

Figure 5-1A is a squared face and squared end, rebated wrought stone (ashlar), which is used as a quoin in stonework. Figure 5-1B is a squared rough-faced ashlar and Fig. 5-1C is an axed ashlar. Figure 5-2A is a boasted edge while Fig. 5-2B is a tool-axed dressed stone. The drafts can be either slanted or perpendicular. A fully wrought stone may have to be shortened during stonework, to fit the place in which it is to be set. Figure 5-3A is a vermiculated stone, finished with small points. Chisels are sunk in to a depth of ½ inch in an irregular pattern. Figure 5-3B is a rustic quoin. This wrought stone is finished with small points and chisels in a random fashion, giving it a worm-eaten appearance.

Figure 5-4A is a broached, face-dressed stone, finished with a point. The point forms a furrow with rough edges as it is worked across the stone's face at the required angle. Figure 5-4B is a picked,

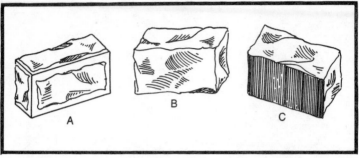

Fig. 5-1. Examples of wrought stones. (A) is rebated ashlar stone and (B) is rough-faced ashlar stone. (C) is axed ashlar.

faced stone, having a projecting reveal. It is made with a chisel and punch.

Figure 5-5A is a natural quarry stone, squared and pitched with a chisel and hammer. This stone is used in very rustic natural ashlar

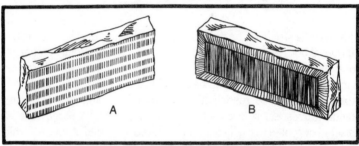

Fig. 5-2. (A) has been boasted and (B) has been tool-axed.

stonework. Figure 5-5B is a crossdressed stone which is cross-worked with a bush hammer. It can be worked to a fine finish, if it is soft stone, by rubbing the face with sand and water. Then it is called plain ashlar. Some ashlar-face dresses are sunk to a depth of ½ inch, leaving a ½ to 1-inch wide arris edge protruding.

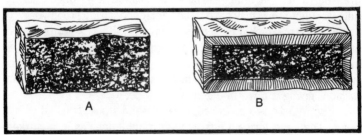

Fig. 5-3. (A) is vermiculated stone. (B) is sunken stone.

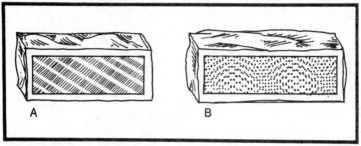

Fig. 5-4. (A) is broached,rebated stone. (B) is picked, faced stone.

MACHINERY

To a very large extent, machinery has taken over the sizing, dressing and shaping of stone used in stonework. Powered hand tools can do carving, edging, cutting, drilling, chipping, bush hammering, etc. Surfacing machines rough down stone to almost any finish. Grinding machines prepare a stone surface for polishing. Disc-cutting and polishing lathes are also used to shape and finish stone. Sand-blasting renews the appearance of stonework.

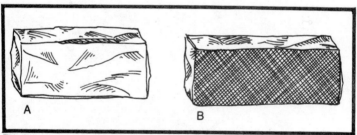

Fig. 5-5. (A) is natural quarry stone. (B) is cross-dressed stone.

Almost any wrought stone may be purchased. Rustic or split-face ashlar, with top and bottom beds sawed, requires only its ends to be cut, sawed, or broken to length. It may be purchased in various depths and breadths in multiples of 2¼, 5, or 7¾ inches or more in breadth, which allow bonding with brick or other backing-up units. Lengths of sawed stone vary from 1 to 5 feet.

MACHINERY

Chapter 6
Mortar

Today, *mortar* is just about as essential as stone in stonework. When the colossal monuments were built by the Egyptians (3733 B.C.) and the Greeks used stone for Gothic architecture, mortar was not used. The stone was wrought so that it would fit into stonework so closely that mortar was unnecessary.

Mortar, it is said, holds the stone apart. It is also said that mortar sticks the stone together. But the purpose of mortar is to fill all voids between the stones in stonework. The essential materials needed to make mortar are binder, aggregate, water and color, if desired.

BINDERS

The binders used in stonemasonry mortars are principally cements, limes and their combinations.

Cement

Cement is one of the strongest binders used in stone mortar. There are other kinds of cements: *natural cement, Portland cement, Keen cement, etc.*

The natural cement is slower setting and not as hard and strong as Portland cement. It is made from argillaceous limestone. The percentages of this stone's ingredients vary, so cement made from this rock is low in strength and can be used only when quality does not matter.

Fig. 6-1. The immersion method of slaking lime requires the lime to be put in a gunny sack and placed in water.

Portland cement is manufactured from limestone, shale and clay, with proportions kept constant by testing. Its quality is uniform as to desired specifications. When made from cement rock, the same adjustments by testing are practiced. Raw materials are calcined and then pulverized into powdered Portland cement of the grade desired.

Lime

The finest metamorphic state of *lime* is white marble. When properly burned, pure lime with a small amount of impurities forms quicklime which, when properly slaked, increases in size and emits a considerable amount of heat. It forms, with the addition of water, a paste of calcium hydroxide or hydrate, and is known as lime putty. If it has great activity in slaking, it is called fat-lime. When quicklime is properly slaked with water and then evaporated, it becomes a powder called hydrated lime.

METHODS OF SLAKING QUICKLIME

In slaking, quicklime will generally absorb about two-thirds its volume of water. There are three ways to slake quicklime: the *sprinkling method, immersion method* and the *drowning method.*

Immersion Method

In the immersion method, the lime is put in a porous container, such as a gunny sack, and suspended in water until it absorbs the necessary quantity of water. Lime will take up just so much water. It is then set aside to dry into a powder. (Fig. 6-1)

Drowning Method

In the drowning method of slaking lime, the lime is spread out in a box to a depth of 6 inches. It is then flooded with water-and allowed to stand and absorb the water until slaked. The lime should not be disturbed until the slaking process is complete, which can take several days. Should it be disturbed, the slaking process may stop. The result will be lime putty instead of a powdered lime. (Fig. 6-2)

Sprinkling Method

In the sprinkling method, the lime is sifted or sprinkled into the water until all the water is taken up by the lime. The best results occur when the depth of the lime comes to 8 inches in the box. (Fig. 6-3)

HYDRATED LIME

Hydrated lime has the property of being able to set and harden under water when mortar is made from it. It makes a good binder. This processed lime, made from limestone containing principally carbonate of lime with carbonate of magnesia and clay (silica), can be used alone or mixed with cements when making mortar. The best source is stone containing 15 to 25 percent clay when carbonate of

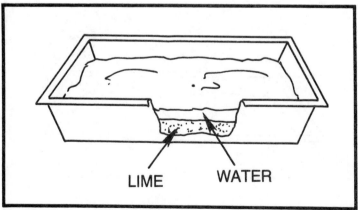

LIME   WATER

Fig. 6-2. Lime is flooded with water in the drowning method.

magnesia is lacking. It should be burned or calcined to a complete fusion of the silicate of lime. By calcining at as low a temperature as practicable so as not to stop the evolution, clinkers are formed which will harden under water when slaked with water and used as a binder in a mix. The clinkers can be ground and pulverized.

Hydrated lime can be used as is or made into a putty and put in a mix. Either way, the lime can be combined with cement and used as a binder in a mortar mix. When used with cement, the mortar will set harder and sustain a heavier load than when cement is not added.

There are other binders, such as asphalt, tar, pitch common cements, etc. I have not used these in stonework mortars.

Color

The best color to use in mortar when colored mortar joints are desired is a mineral oxide color. It can be procured in many colors. Any color used should be of a non-fade type and of a color strength that will not require a quantity in excess of 10 percent of the binder used.

Water

Only good, clean, drinkable water should be used when making mortar for stonework. It should be free from alkalines, acids, oils, sulfurs and salts. Sea water should not be used because the salt in it attracts moisture and keeps the mortar in the stonework joints continually damp. Furthermore, only a quantity of water shall be used to begin the action of the binder. Stone mortar should be stiff,

Fig. 6-3. Lime is sprinkled into water in the sprinkling method.

plastic mortar and not thin, sloppy mortar. Mortar for some kinds of porous stone can be much thinner and not so stiff, or else the stones should be well wetted before setting.

AGGREGATE

An *aggregate* is often an essential ingredient in mortar. There are three kinds or classifications of aggregates. There are natural aggregates, artificial aggregates and fibrous aggregates.

Natural Aggregates

In the natural aggregate classification are sand, gravel, crushed rock, stone, granite, marble, shells, slate, pumice, shale, etc. . All have to be sized, graded, and, if necessary, washed to rid them of impurities.

Artificial Aggregates

Artificial aggregates are broken or crushed brick and clay units, ashes, glass, artificial slag artificial chips, pottery, iron fillings, clinkers, etc. All of these will have to be sized, and possibly washed. They can be used with natural aggregates, if desired.

Fibrous Aggregates

The fibrous aggregates include wool fiber, reeds, cork, hair, straw, hay, wood, shavings, sawdust (treated against moisture), etc. These aggregates are seldom used today in stonework mortars, except in special instances or in combination with natural or artificial aggregates.

Sized Aggregate

Aggregates should be sized or graded from very fine to coarse. This will insure the use of less binder and a stronger, void-free stonework mortar.

Very fine aggregate will pass through a number 30 hole in a square inch screen (or number 30 sieve). Fine aggregate will pass through a screen having ¼-inch holes.

Aggregates should have a mixture of very fine, fine and coarse grades. A well-graded aggregate should have 95 percent mixture of veryl-graded aggregate should have 95 percent of its particles pass through a number eight screen, 65 percent pass through a number 16 screen, 30 percent go through a number 30 screen, 20 percent pass through a number 50 screen, and not more than 10 percent filter through a number 100 screen. These percentages will vary some. Should fine aggregates be more numerous more water will be required in the mortar mix. This will result in weaker mortar. If the coarser aggregate is very prevalent in the graded aggregate, the mortar will be grainy, hard to handle, less waterproof and less weather-resistant. It will also require more binder in the mix.

All aggregates used should be free of impurities, such as clay, loam, silt, vegetable matter, salt, sulfur, acid, alkali, etc.. Most aggregates are found with other material and are of varying size and quality. It is necessary, when making first class stonework mortar, to test the aggregate for quality and grade if it is not known, or if it is not taken from a place known to yield a qualified aggregate.

Percentages of silt, clay, and loam in an aggregate may be found by placing the aggregate sample in a pint jar to a depth of 2 inches. Then fill the jar with good water within an inch or so of the top. Shake the jar well and let it stand until the water is clear. Should a ⅛-inch layer of silt or loam appear on the top of the aggregate, the aggregate should be washed. Also, the same amount of aggregate in the above test can be used when testing for impurities in the aggregate. Just add a level tablespoon of common lye to the water. After it sets for 24 hours or so, the aggregate should be washed if the water is darker than the straw color of apple cider vinegar. Aggregate containing sulfur, which is easily detected by its smell and color, should be washed possibly more than once to rid it of sulfur.

Careful selection of aggregate is a must when good strength, durability, fire resistance, lightness, retention of water during its plastic stage, or where a combination of these are imperative. Combinations of two or more aggregates may be required for their compressive or tensile strengths. Cost may be increased or decreased with respect to the mortar for the type of stonework in which it is to be used. All added aggregate should, if possible, be equal in quality or harder and more durable than any particle of the mix it enters, if strength is desired. Any additive that naturally weakens a mix below its requirements should be used, even though it costs less.

MAKING MORTAR

Mortar should be made with clean tools, whether with hand or power tools (mixers). Mortar should be covered in rainy weather, and kept from freezing in cold weather. Water used when making mortar should not be boiling or overly hot; nor should there be ice in the water.

When making morter, the materials used should be waterproof and non-fading, especially for stonework mortar. Non-staining binders should be used, especially for outside stonework. It is best not to temper stonework mortars. They should be discarded when they have lost their plasticity and are hard to handle or semi-set. Some stonework requires a grout-like mortar. For most stonework, a plastic, heavy thick mortar, with just enough water in it to start the chemical action of the binder, is pertinent to good mortar.

Hand-Mixed Mortar

When mixing mortar by hand, the aggregate is put in a mixing box and leveled off with a hoe. Measure the dry materials with the measuring box. The binder is spread out over the aggregate. Color, if required is scattered over the binder. The hoe is now used to put the materials together. Make sure the ingredients are uniformly mixed. Water is now sparingly added and mixed in with the hoe until the required stiffness and consistency of the mix is attained.

Grout is a thin, mix and the aggregate used is very fine. The same method can be employed when mixing grout. Grout is generally mixed in small quantities. The tub is a handy box in which to mix grout. A fire-clay mix is of cream consistency and the tub comes in handy in its mixing, too.

Power-Mixed Mortar

There are several power mixers on the market. The paddle kind is one of the best. The aggregate is put in the mixer along with the binder, color and water. I put some of the water and aggregate into the mixer for starters. I add the rest with care. Be careful not to get too much water. A sloppy mortar is seldom desirable. Whether you use hand-mixed or power-mixed mortar, all aggregate should have each particle covered with binder in order to have well-mixed, uniform mortar.

There are load-bearing mortars and non-load-bearing mortars. The best load-bearing mortars have Portland cement as a binder. Non-bearing mortars have cement and lime in various proportions as a binder. A good load-bearing mortar consists of one part Portland cement and one part to 2½ parts well-graded sand, plus color if desired. Use enough water to bring the mix to the consistency desired. Another good load-bearing mortar consists of one part good white cement to 2½ to 3 parts of graded aggregate. Add as much water as is necessary. Color can be added to the binder if required. Non-load-bearing mortars can consist of the following ingredients as per the four mixes, from strongest to weakest mortar:

- **Mix one**. Portland cement, 1 part; lime, 10 to 15 percent of one part; graded sand, three parts; color, if necessary; and water as necessary.
- **Mix two**. Portland or white cement; 1 part; lime, ¼ part; graded sand, 4 parts; color, if needed; and water as necessary.
- **Mix three**. Cement, 1 part; lime, ½ part; graded sand, 4 parts; color, if needed; and water as necessary.
- **Mix four**. Cement, 1 part; lime, 1 part; graded sand, 4 parts color, if needed; and water as necessary.
- **Mix five**. Cement, 1 part; lime, 2 parts; graded sand, 6 to 7 parts; color, if needed; and water as necessary.
- **Mix six**. Lime, 1 part; graded sand, 5 to 6 parts; color, if needed, and water as necessary.

Sometimes the stone used sucks the moisture from the mortar before it can set. In this case the stone should be well wetted before the mortar is placed on its bed, whether it is thick or thin mortar.

Chapter 7
Bonds of Stonework

Stonework may be classified with respect to the shape of the stone used. Certain shaped stone is best used in one or more of the distinctive kinds (bonds) of stonework. These bonds are *cobble, rubble, ashlar* and *decorative*. Then there is a mixture of these kinds, mostly the work of amateur stone setters. This so-called "catch-as-catch-can" method of picking up stone and setting it randomly in stonework follows no method of uniformity and is a mess. Such stonework has little strength.

I consider any stone, whether shaped or wrought, having true or regular arris bed lines as rubble stock. Any stone shaped or wrought to a straight plane or line and squared at its face arrises is designated as ashlar stock. I consider most fieldstone as cobble stock. Some stone will be usable in diaper-like pattern panels in decorative stonework.

STYLES AND PATTERNS

Within each classification of stonework, there are systematic styles or bonds and patterns. These styles are *random* or *range, coursed* and *random coursed*. However, the true ashlar bond of stonework holds true to a pattern when setting its stone.

There is no systematized arrangement when setting stone, whether cobble, rubble or ashlar, in the random range style.

In the coursed, block coursed and random coursed styles, I stay within bonds of the courses. These bonds extend throughout the

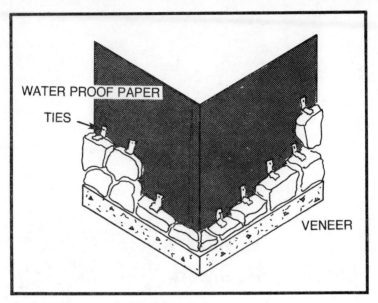

Fig. 7-1. Rubble veneer is used often.

length of the stonework, whether cobble, rubble or ashlar stonework.

Regarding the coursed style, stones are of the same breadth face, but may vary in length and depth. It is not necessary that all courses be of the same breadth.

In the block coursed style, stones may vary in width. But the stone breadths should add up to the breadth of the largest stone breadth in the course, which may be 8 to 20 inches. The lengths of stone in this stonework may vary.

In the course of the random coursed style, stones vary in breadth, length, and depth. But they stay within the coursed style, which may vary from 12 to 20 inches in breadth from one horizontal course to the other.

The styles may be used alone or in combination with the other styles in the random coursed style bond. But they are at no less than 4 to 5-foot lengths. No horizontal bed joint of a course should be less than 5 feet long. No course should end in alignment with any other course. Perpendicular head joints of the courses should not be over any other of a course. Courses should always lap over head joints. This holds true whether the stonework is cobble, rubble or ashlar.

Decorative stonework may be of stone combinations with respect to size, color, kind, dress or finish, including carved and scroll, as well as diaper-like patterns. The stonework may present itself in

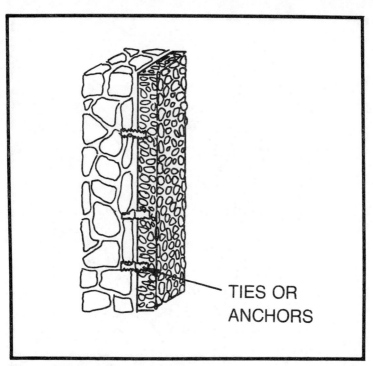

Fig. 7-2. Cobble veneer with stone backing.

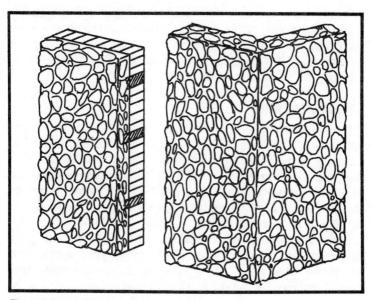

Fig. 7-3. Cobble veneer with brick backing.

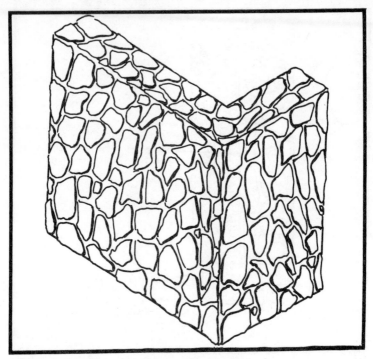

Fig. 7-4. Split cobble can be laid as rubble stonework.

colored mortar, as well as one of the various styles of mortar joints. It can be of cobble, rubble or ashlar stone. Repeat patterns are not too complicated and can be mastered. Size and color of stone will enhance many pattern designs. Patterned stonework can be rustic, whether the stone is wrought or natural.

COBBLE STONEWORK

Cobblestone is used in residential construction to lend a rustic appearance. Cobblestones (fieldstones) vary in size from 4 to 20 inches in diameter, and are somewhat rounded and smaller than boulders. This stone does not require splitting or pitching when used in cobble stonework. The stone is random set. However, a pattern may be used. Then, too, cobble stonework requires some sort of backing. It is principally used as a veneer (Fig. 7-1).

Cobblestones can be split and set with the split face out. They can be pitched after splitting to fit in stonework more closely. Split and pitched stonework, with cobblestone, has an appearance of a cobweb and could be called cobweb stonework. Cobweb stonework can act as a veneer because it requires backing (Figs. 7-2 and 7-3).

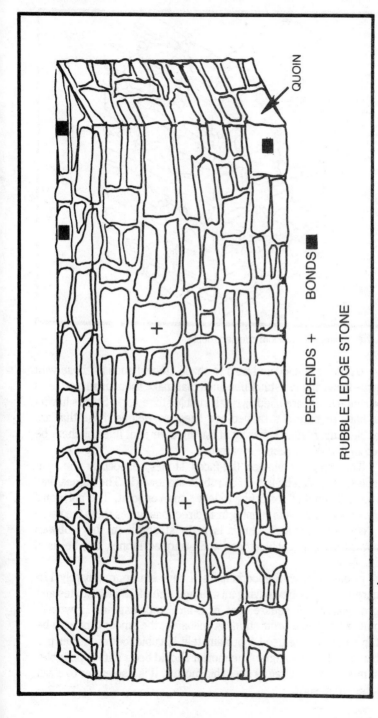

QUOIN

PERPENDS +   BONDS ■

RUBBLE LEDGE STONE

Fig. 7-5. Uncoursed rubble stonework consists of unsquared, semi-squared, roughly worked and ledge stone.

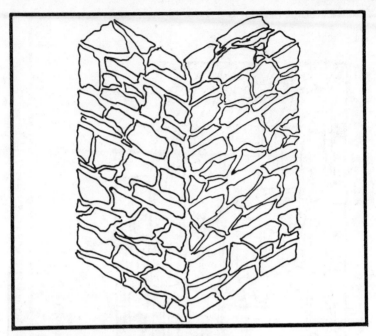

Fig. 7-6. Example of random coursed rubble.

Irregular shaped and hard to shape stones, such as those with untrue faces and indistinct bed lines that make them unadaptable to horizontal beds, are used as rustic rubble stonework. Stones having bed lines or natural stratified bed lines, as well as those that are scabbled, may, after squaring or having their joint lines pitched, be used in first-class rubble stonework.

The irregular shaped flat-faced stones, especially the split cobblestones, can be laid up as rubble stonework. The stones may be partially pitched for fitting to leave an even joint. The polygonal appearance with joints running in all directions, gives them the name of "cobweb rubble." There is little strength in this cobweb stonework. Split cobblestones and stratified stones can be used (Fig. 7-4).

In one day, with good helpers, I have set approximately 115 square feet of cobble, having an average size of 12-inch stones and approximately 75 square feet of 8-inch cobblestone. However, temperature and mortar stiffness will affect the amount that can be set in a day. I have used approximately ¼ cubic foot of mortar per cubic foot of cobblestone. The mortar should be as stiff as possible. Stiff mortar will not sag as does thin mortar. It is also easier to clean off the stonework.

RUBBLE STONEWORK

Uncoursed rubble stonework is formed with unsquared, irregular shaped, and rather rough surface stone, as well as semi-squared roughly or pitched stone and ledge stone (Fig. 7-5). In the course of the random-coursed rubble, stones vary in breadth, length and depth (Fig. 7-6). But they stay within the bounds of the course, which may be 12 to 20 inches in breadth from one horizontal bed joint to another.

In the random-coursed bond, the bond may be used alone or in combination with other bonds. But they are broken at 4 to 5-foot lengths, as no horizontal bed joint is longer than 5 lineal feet. This holds true, whether the stonework is cobble, rubble or ashlar (Figs. 7-7 and 7-8).

Range or range-coursed, coursed, and their variations are formed with practically any stone, whether worked or not worked,

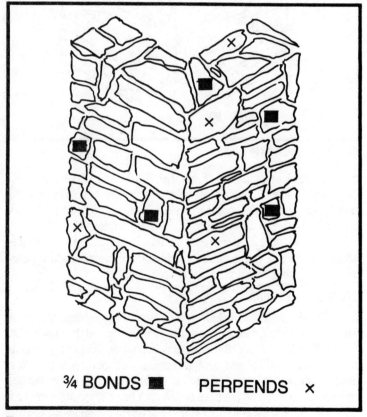

¾ BONDS ■   PERPENDS ✕

Fig. 7-7. Ledge random rubble.

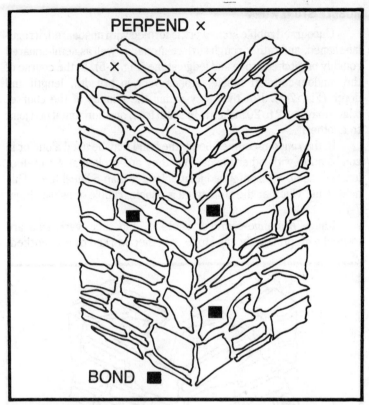

PERPEND ×

BOND ■

Fig. 7-8. Broken course rubble.

or of equal or unequal size (Figs. 7-9, 7-10, 7-11, 7-12 and 7-13). Stratified stone of various sizes and breadths will bring up the transverse bed joint comparatively level, which will make a stronger, better bonded and more durable stonework.

Snecked rubble stonework can be used in coursed rubble stonework. Or it can maintain its random semi-patterned appearance throughout the stonework (Fig. 7-14).

BLOCKING METHODS

Blocking methods include setting two stones against one, three stones against one, two stones against three, etc. All the stones may be of different lengths and are set against snecks, jumpers, perpends or course stones. Other than appearance, a jumper's only benefit in stonework is that it forms a vertical tie between two more courses. Bonds, perpends and jumpers break up a brick-bond appearance in stonework. Too many jumpers used will weaken stonework and may cause a diagonal rupture.

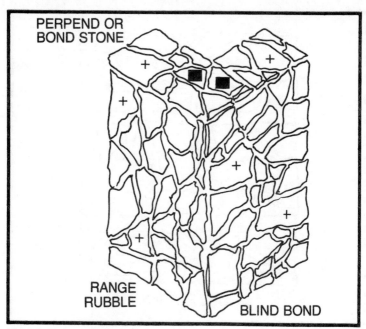

Fig. 7-9. Range rubble.

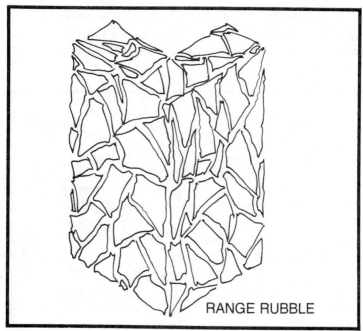

Fig. 7-10. Another variety of range rubble.

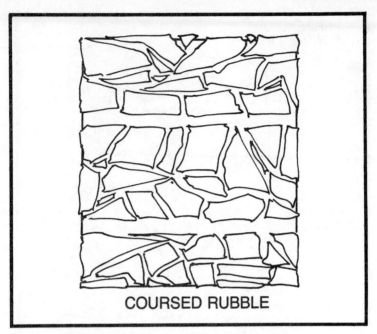

COURSED RUBBLE

Fig. 7-11. Coursed rubble can be formed with stones of unequal size.

In most rubble stonework, I find it best to use various sizes of stones and strive for irregularity. However, the larger size stones should be set near the bottom of a stonework wall rather than at the top (Fig. 7-15).

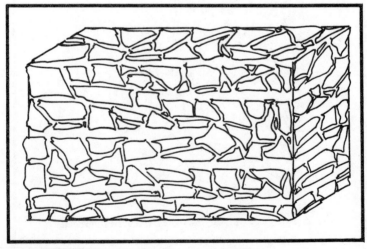

Fig. 7-12. Another example of random coursed rubble.

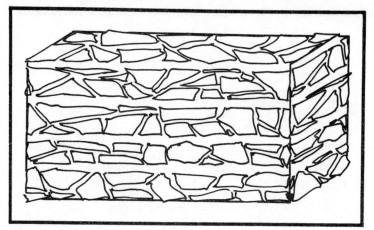

Fig. 7-13. Coursed rubble.

Should a semi-rustic appearance be desired, the stone may require some shaping with a hammer (Fig. 7-16). Stone may need pitching. It may require the use of a point or bush hammer. If a very rustic appearance is desired, the stone is not shaped or otherwise worked. No selection of size or shape is required as all voids on the face of the stonework are either filled with mortar or chinked with spalls.

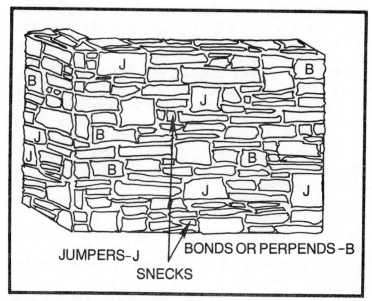

JUMPERS–J   BONDS OR PERPENDS –B
SNECKS

Fig. 7-14. Snecked rubble stonework.

Fig. 7-15. Blocked rubble.

With good helpers, I can handle and set approximately 75 cubic feet of rubble stonework in a 16-inch thick wall. I can also do approximately 95 cubic feet of rustic rubble stonework, in a 30-inch wall, in one working day. It will take approximately ¼ cubic foot of mortar to set 1 cubic foot of rubble stonework.

Rubble stonework formed from semi-squared, shaped and worked stone, especially stratified stone, is considered to be the best rubble stonework, or the most rustic ashlar stonework. This kind of stonework may be considered the last step that introduces the ashlar stonework.

With good helpers, I can handle, pitch, and set approximately 70 square feet of very rustic cobweb rubble stonework in one working day, using stone averaging 12-inches across the face, of sizes from 8 to 14 inches. When the average is 16 inches, I can handle, hammer-pitch and set 100 square feet in one working day. Where less rustication is desired, the amount of stonework per day will be regulated primarily by the average size of the stone used. It will take approximately ¼ cubic foot of mortar per cubic foot of stone. I am always concerned with the spilling of mortar. The stonework should be kept as clean as possible.

I can handle and set approximately 75 cubic feet of rustic rubble stonework in a 30-inch thick wall, in one working day. I will use approximately ¼ cubic foot of mortar to set a cubic foot of rubble stonework.

Rubble stonework with a square or oblong face can be formed from semi-squared, shaped and worked stone. This type is considered by some stonemasons as the best rubble stonework or the most rustic ashlar stonework.

This stone is obtainable from manufacturers and mills in any finish and grade, as well as size and shape. It may be finished on one side or on all sides. It may be beveled, guttered, tooled, scrolled or wrought in any of the finishes desired. This stone will require little handwork, as it is ordered to fit the place in which it will be set.

The setting of this stone is done with cement mortar. The joints are small, generally no larger than ⅛-inch are wiped rather than struck or tooled with jointers on inside work. On outside settings, the joints can be thicker and tooled. The sand used is fine to very fine. White sand is best. Cement should be of the best stain-resistant white or Portland cement, colored or natural. The stone is well-wetted with water just before applying the mortar and setting. The mortar is rich—1 part cement to 1 to 2 parts and color, if desired. It should be mixed to a heavy grout consistency using drinkable water.

Some stone is set in stonework with other material such as brick, tile and block as backing, or in combination with other stones. It is necessary to procure stone of a size which will fit with these other materials, when incorporated in the stonework combinations.

Stones should be purchased which are of sizes that can be used with other building units. Otherwise, the stones will need to be shaped by hand on the job to fit. The most common sizes are 2¼, 5, 7¾, or 10 inches in breadth. The length can be as is or cut on the job.

The quantity of stone needed for stonework is generally arrived at by multiplying the height. by the length by the depth of the stonework, less the openings, which gives the cubic feet required.

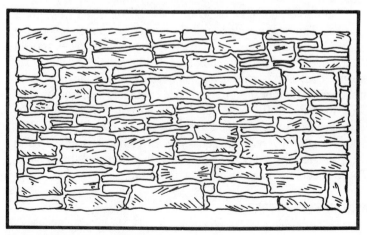

Fig. 7-16. Hammer-squared stone.

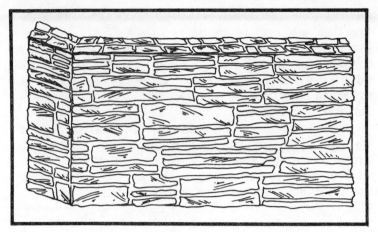

Fig. 7-17. Rusticated ashlar stone is very rough.

This cubic foot quantity, if purchased by the yard, is divided by 27 to find the yards needed. If purchased by the perch, divide the cubic feet by 16½ to find the number of perches required. When bought by the ton, multiply the cubic feet by the weight of a cubic foot of stone (check the material weight tables in this book) and divide by 2000 to arrive at the tons required.

Vertical joints (head joints) should be broken, and not one over the other, unless the pattern used designates otherwise. Bed joints should conform to the types of stonework and be broken whenever possible. Cracks in stonework nearly always follow through the joints in the style of laying whether cobble, rubble, ashlar or patterned.

The stone should be of good quality and of equal strength, if possible. The weakest stone will always crack or crush before the strong. Stone should also be set in a job, whenever possible, with its natural bed on the bed joint in order to withstand the greatest load weight. I am always careful when choosing stone for any particular stonework, whether the job is an inside or outside job. Stone is soft, hard, medium, brittle or tough. It may have a cleavage plane, no cleavage plane or be stratified. Stone can also be porous, solid, fine, coarse-textured or mixed in density when a stone is stratified. With care, all building stone can be shaped with power tools or by hand. There should be no voids left in stonework.

ASHLAR STONEWORK

Ashlar stonework is employed in practically any structure where stone is used. It can be any style or pattern, whether struc-

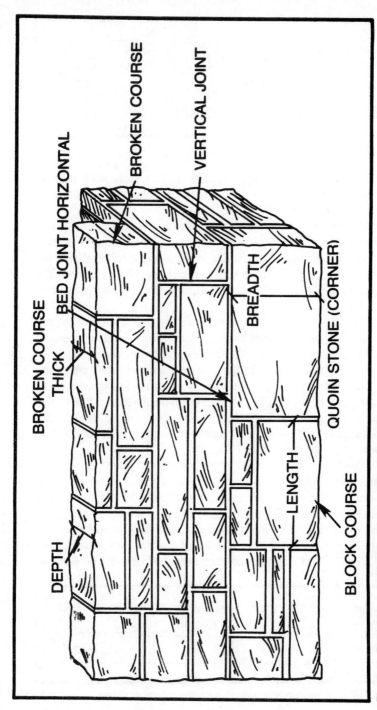

BROKEN COURSE

BROKEN COURSE

VERTICAL JOINT

BED JOINT HORIZONTAL

THICK

BREADTH

DEPTH

QUOIN STONE (CORNER)

LENGTH

BLOCK COURSE

Fig. 7-18. Block course ashlar has courses of varying widths.

Fig. 7-19. Random coursed ashlar.

tural, decorative, interior or outside. Ashlar stonework may be rustic, rusticated or dressed and, in some instances, polished to a mirror-like finish.

Ashlar stonework is principally used as a veneer and is seldom more than 4 to 6 inches thick. As a structural stonework, it is at least 8 inches thick, unless its backing is such that it will sustain itself under a load. Ashlar stone is still used in the regular 8 inch breadths and up to 5 feet long. The stone breadths vary in sizes from an inch up.

This stonework comprises many different methods of arranging stone, such as rusticated ashlar, block coursed ashlar, random coursed ashlar, coursed ashlar, random course of coursed style or bond, patterned ashlar, broken pattern and repeated patterned ashlar. Rusticated ashlar stonework may partially follow any pattern (bond) of stonework. It is very rough and need not hold true to any level bed (Fig. 7-17). Block course ashlar stonework has different width courses with different breadths and lengths of ashlar stone in blocks in the courses (Fig. 7-18).

Random coursed ashlar stonework may be of any style or bond—two stones to one, two stones to three, etc (Fig. 7-19). Coursed ashlar stonework may have different length stones in a course (Fig. 7-20). However, the course generally is the same breadth throughout its length. This style (bond) of ashlar stonework is uniform and gives the appearance of solidarity, especially if the ashlar stone is of the same size and is drafted (Fig. 7-21). Random

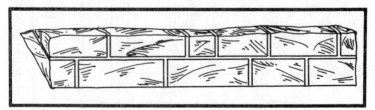

Fig. 7-20. Coursed ashlar stonework has different length stones.

96

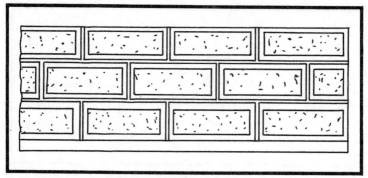

Fig. 7-21. Coursed drafted ashlar stonework.

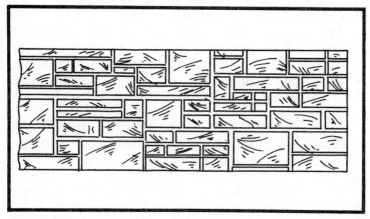

Fig. 7-22. Random course of coursed ashlar stonework does not have a uniform bond.

Fig. 7-23. Pattern design ashlar stonework has a uniform pattern.

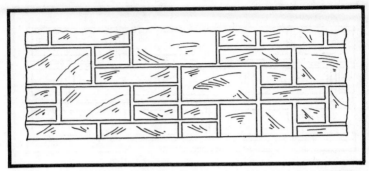

Fig. 7-24. The ashlar stones in this stonework have no continuous bed joint.

course of coursed ashlar stonework has different size ashlar stones set without a uniform style (bond) (Fig. 7-22).

Patterned ashlar stonework has a pattern in it which is carried and adhered to throughout the stonework (Fig. 7-23). The pattern may be two ashlar stones to one, one to three, etc. Also, there can be certain uniform settings of stone in a pattern which hold true continuously in the ashlar stonework. The vertical joints hold true in this pattern.

In the broken pattern ashlar stonework, the ashlar stones are even sized in length, having no continuous bed joint. This stonework has a rather monotonous appearance, but it is strong and durable (Fig. 7-24).

Repeated patterned ashlar stonework is a continuous pattern such that the pattern and bond followed will fit one another. There are different courses of pattern bond ashlar stonework (Figs. 7-25, 7-26 and 7-27).

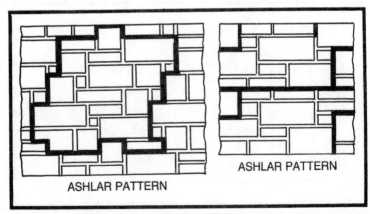

ASHLAR PATTERN

ASHLAR PATTERN

Fig. 7-25. Repeated patterned ashlar stonework.

Sanded and polished ashlar stone is generally used in ashlar stonework for business building fronts and insides of some public buildings (Figs. 7-28 and 7-29). The ashlar stone is generally wrought in stone plants, either of quarry stone or fabricated stone (artificial stone). It can be veneer stonework, having backing of stone, brick, tile or manufactured block. Concrete is also a backing.

This ashlar stone can be bought from stone manufacturers and mills in any finish or size and shape desired. Its finish may be a sawed, rubbed, honed, polished or rusticated face. The store may

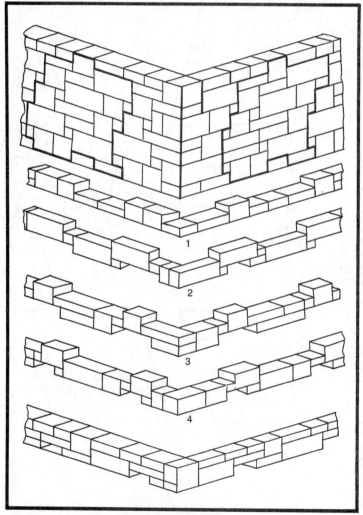

Fig. 7-26. Courses of pattern bond ashlar.

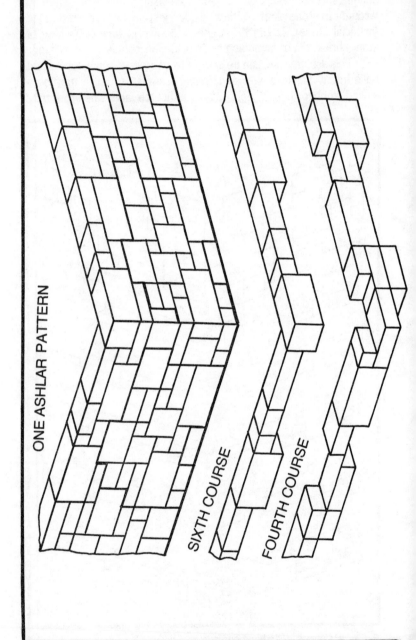

ONE ASHLAR PATTERN

SIXTH COURSE

FOURTH COURSE

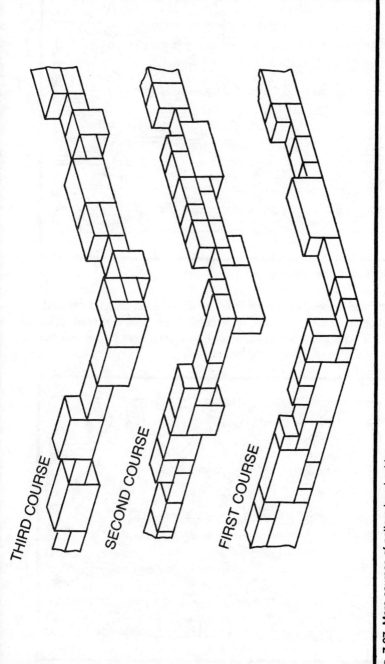

THIRD COURSE

SECOND COURSE

FIRST COURSE

Fig. 7-27. More courses of pattern bond ashlar.

101

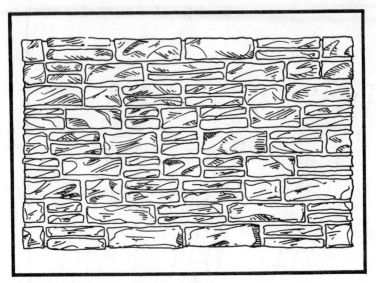

Fig. 7-28. A rustic ashlar pattern.

be hand-finished on one side or on all sides. It may be beveled, guttered, tooled, scrolled, or wrought in any shape or finish (Fig. 7-30). This ashlar stone will require little hand work as it is ordered to fit the places in which it will be set.

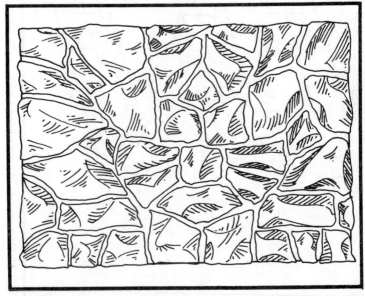

Fig. 7-29. Rubble patterned stonework.

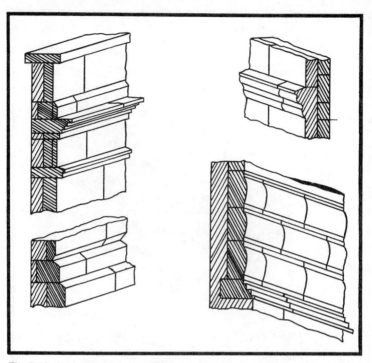

Fig. 7-30. Ashlar may be wrought and sanded into various shapes.

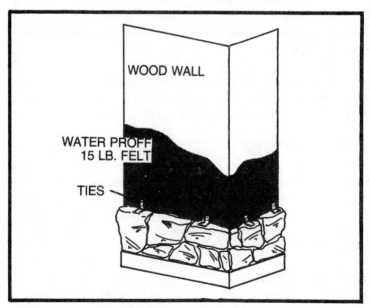

WOOD WALL

WATER PROFF
15 LB. FELT

TIES

Fig. 7-31. Rubble veneer stonework.

103

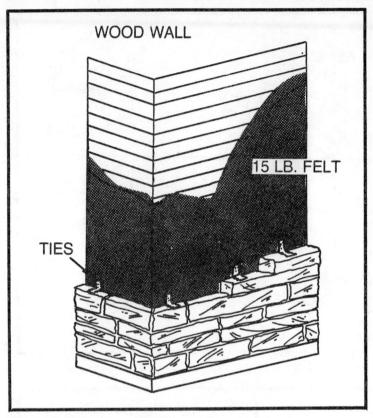

WOOD WALL

15 LB. FELT

TIES

Fig. 7-32. Ashlar veneer stonework.

It will save considerable work if sizes are ordered that will fit such backing as is intended for use. The most common breadth sizes are 2¼, 5, 7¾ or 10 inches. The lengths can be as is or cut on the job.

DECORATIVE STONEWORK

Decorative stonework may be of any stone combinations with respect to size, color, kind, dress or finish, including carved and scroll stonework. It may present itself in colored mortar, as well as various kinds of mortar joints. It can be of cobble, rubble or ashlar stonework. Further, patterned designs can contain as many different combinations and bonds as does brickwork.

VENEER STONEWORK

Veneer needs a solid foundation on which to set. *Veneer stonework* should be fastened with ties to whatever it veneers. The ties must be approximately 16 inches apart, either fastened to the wall against which the stone is set or embedded in the backing. There should be a seal, asphalt paper or a water seal between the stonework and that to which it is fastened. This will keep moisture from passing from one to the other.

Veneer can be either of cobble stonework, rubble stonework, ashlar stonework or pattern stonework.

Stone veneer generally needs at least a 5-inch depth in which to set. The stone can vary in depth from 2½ to 4½ inches whether cobble, rubble, ashlar or diaper-like patterned decorative panels (Figs. 7-31 and 7-32).

Chapter 8
Stone Setting

Before stone can be set, it is necessary to have a good foundation and place to put stonework. When a location is found, the layout can take place. Surveying is generally performed by a professional surveyor. Zoning, health regulations, local and state laws and possibly a building permit, will have to be looked into and complied with accordingly. After these matters are taken care of, then stakes, batten boards and lines can be used to layout the building.

After the corner stake is established—and the grade found, the stakes to hold the batten boards can be driven (Fig. 8-1). With a large square and diagonal measurements, the squareness of the building can be determined. All the batten boards should be level with each other if possible. Measuring down from the guide lines will help to keep the building to grade.

After excavation, the footings can be placed in stone or poured with concrete. All stone footings should rest on solid soil, clay, tamped gravel or bedrock.

Footings should be level, especially the top of footings (Fig.8-2). They can be reinforced with reinforcing bars (re-bars). Footings put on solid beds are considered good if they are below frost line, and are in width twice that of the foundation or wall that sets on it. The depth of the footing should equal the width of the wall, plus the width of the footing, when setting on a good bed or a well-tamped gravel bed. Footing should extend equally on each side of the foundation or wall that sets on it. If possible, I make footings wider at the corners of buildings. This action keeps walls of buildings from cracking from the top down.

QUANTITY OF STONE NEEDED

The quantity of stone needed for stonework will have to be delivered to the site. Binder, aggregate, color and water should be at the site. Such tools as needed should be at hand. A hodcarrier and mortar man should be ready when stone laying starts. Also, you, the stonemason, should be ready to set the stone you have wrought, sized, shaped, dressed, etc.

To figure the quantity of stone, multiply the breadth by the length by the depth of stonework to be set, less openings which gives the cubic feet required. Don't forget to add the percentage for wroughting, which may vary as much as from 6 percent to 15 percent.

If stone is purchased by the cubic yard, divide this cubic quantity by 27 to get the yards needed. If purchased by the perch, divide by 16½ to find the perches required. When ordered by the ton, multiply the cubic foot of stone by the weight of the cubic foot of the kind of stone for the job. Divide by 2000 to arrive at the tons required. (The cubic foot weight of stone can be found in tables near the end of this book). All these quantities will require a percentage to be added for waste when the stone is wrought on the job.

Stone used in stonework should be of good quality and of equal strength, if possible. Stone should always be set in stonework with its natural bed joint on the bed joint, in order to better withstand the greatest load weight. The weakest stone will always crack or crush before the strong. I always am careful when choosing stone for any particular job, whether the stonework is for inside or outside. As mentioned before, stone is soft, hard, medium, brittle or tough. Again, it may have a cleavage plane, no cleavage plane or possibly be stratified. This will make it hard or easy to wrought. Stone may be porous, solid, fine or coarse textured, or mixed in density as is a stratified stone. With care, all building stone can be shaped with power tools or by hand.

QUANTITY OF STONE SET

The quantity of stone that can be set for a given time will vary depending on the stone, the bond, where the stonework is to be done, and on the stonemason and helpers. The mortar used has a lot to do with the quantity that can be set. The amount of mortar used can also vary, depending on the stone used, bond laid and the stonemason's wroughting and setting of the stone.

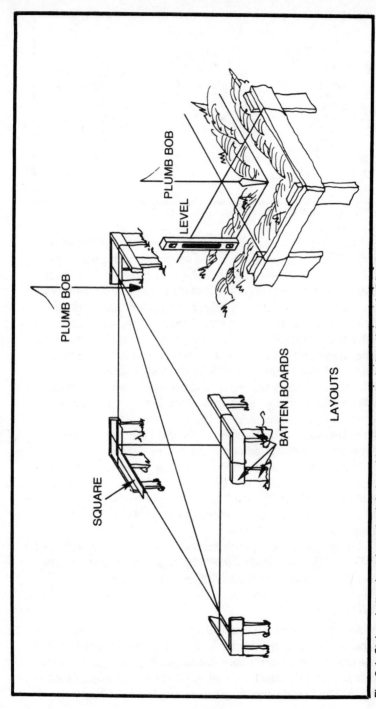

PLUMB BOB

PLUMB BOB

LEVEL

SQUARE

BATTEN BOARDS

LAYOUTS

Fig. 8-1. Stakes, batten boards, a plumb bob and level are required when doing a building layout.

109

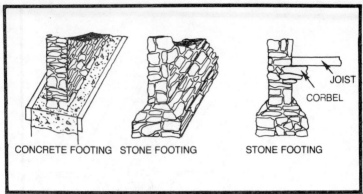

Fig. 8-2. Make sure that footings are level.

I have set over 100 square feet of veneer ashlar stonework in one day. The stone size, pattern, and amount of cutting will vary the quantity of ashlar stonework that can be set in a day. I can set cut and polished ashlar stone much easier than other ashlar stone. However, when a large, heavy stone is used in close-jointed stonework, along with a hoist or derrick, the quantity that can be set will depend to a great extent upon the helpers. The mortar for this kind of stonework will be thin to very thin grout. It will have to be mixed fresh every so often as a straight cement mortar is generally utilized.

A mortar table is needed to hold the mortar when the stone is ready for setting. The building corners are displayed in Fig. 8-1. It is not much of a job to set stone at these corners after the stone and mortar are ready. With the help of the level and mason's line, the stonework can be kept perpendicular and in alignment.

When placing the mortar for setting stone, the mortar is dumped from the trowel onto the mortar bed. Just let it slide from the trowel. The mortar need not be strung out and flared as in brickwork. The mortar bed should have plenty of mortar when setting stone.

The mortar is near grout thinness when setting wrought and polished ashlar, and much thinner when setting polished marble. These mortar joints are from 1/32 to 1/16 inches thick.

MORTAR JOINTS

All bed and vertical or bond joints should be filled. There should not be any voids in the mortar joints. Voids collect moisture and cause cracking and deterioration due to freezing. The excess mortar should be removed with the trowel and the joints properly finished as desired. The jointers for this purpose are found in Chapter 1.

Fig. 8-3. Joggles keep stone in place.

The roughness of stone at the joints do help keep stone in place. Pebbles placed between stone and in the bed mortar also help keep stone from moving out of place.

JOGGLES AND TIES

The stone to be set should have as true a bed plane as possible. It should set in alignment horizontally and be perpendicular with the stonework.

Sometimes wedges are used to right stone. The wedges are pulled out and mortar is forced in to replace them. Some stonemasons use spalls (stone chips) for this purpose. I find it quite handy to use small hardwood wedges for this purpose. Wedges are seldom needed when setting well-wrought ashlar stone.

In stonework, no spall should be left in the stonework, and no stone should be set so it will act as a wedge. This setting will cause the stonework to bulge apart as a result of the weight load. Stone should not slip or slide when set. It should maintain its position under weight load pressures. There are diagonal pressures, lateral motions and tensile strains in all stonework which have to be considered when setting stone. Joggles are sometimes used for the purpose of keeping stone in its proper place, especially when a heavy live or dead load is to be consideed (Figs. 8-3 and 8-4).

There are also ties, re-bars and anchors used to strengthen and help hold stonework in place. Joist ties should be at the bottom of joists. Should a joist break or a fire cause the above part of the building to fall in, the joist anchors will not crack or wreck the stonework (Fig. 8-5).

Fig. 8-4. Examples of joggles and dowels.

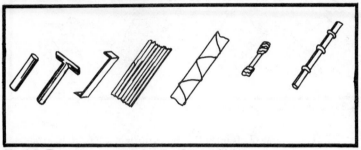
Fig. 8-5. These ties are placed at the bottom of joists.

JOINTS

All joints in stonework should be completely filled with mortar (Fig. 8-6). Where it is not required to finish the joints, they should be brushed crossways with a whisk broom after the protruding mortar is removed with the trowel. The mortar should be semi-set before brushing. The stonework will be less likely to become messy if this is done. Joints that require finishing can either be raked out or tooled with the jointer after brushing. However, if a bead joint is required, it is best to tool it before brushing and use the scutch to clean the mortar off from each side of the mortar bead.

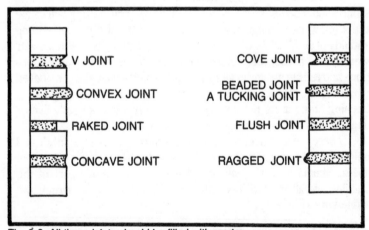
Fig. 8-6. All these joints should be filled with mortar.

When refinishing old joints, I rake them out at least an inch and put in fresh mortar. This mortar can be colored or not and should be, if possible, as strong as the mortar used in the stonework. It should be tucked in and packed in layers by a tucking tool. When filled, it should be tooled with the desired jointer.

Chapter 9
Construction Stones, Parts and Processes

There are names for different parts of stonework as well as names for certain stones used in stonework. Where these stones appear in the line drawings, they are designated. Parts and angles are depicted in Figs. 9-1 through 9-4. Placement of conduits and the reinforcing bars are shown in Fig. 9-5. Anchors nogging, corbeling, toothing and raking are pictured in Figs. 9-6 through 9-11.

PARTITIONS

Different methods are employed when *partitions* are placed after the stone wall or other masonry wall is up (Fig. 9-12). Also, there is a way to join partition walls when they are built as the work progresses.

There are two good ways to join a partition wall to a stonework wall. One method is to drive metal pins into the wall as the partition is made. The other method is to chisel-out insets or pockets in the stonework wall and insert the partition stone as the partition wall is constructed.

BACKING FOR STONEWORK

The *backing* for stonework, if required, should be placed or laid up with the stonework. I use sighting along with a mason's line when setting stone. Two lines come in handy when setting stone whether a required backing is laid, set or just the stone is set without backing. In veneer stone setting I use only one mason's line.

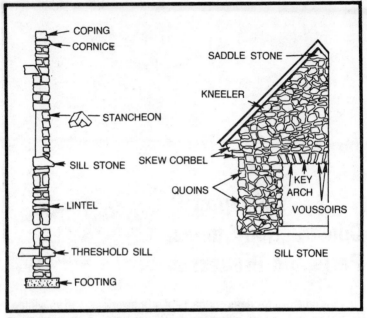

Fig. 9-1. Names of construction parts in stonework.

When the backing is separate from the stonework, as in hollow wall construction, ties are used to hold the wall together or apart. Insulation can fill up the space if desired with either sheet, particle, batting or form insulation (Figs. 9-13 through 9-16).

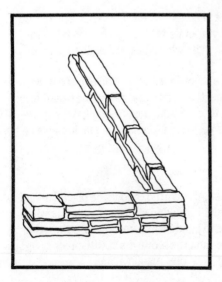

Fig. 9-2. An ashlar acute angle.

114

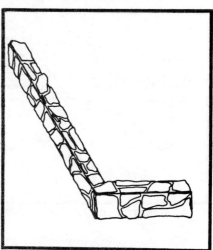

Fig. 9-3. A rubble obtuse angle.

TUCKING

Tucking and cleaning stonework is done on old as well as new stonework. On new stonework, where the mortar joints are raked out or partly filled and require finished joints, tucking is performed (Figs. 9-17 and 9-18). On old work, where the mortar joints have dried out and turned to chalk and sand, or fallen out, tucking is required.

I am always careful to wet the open joints well after raking or cleaning them out to kill the suction.

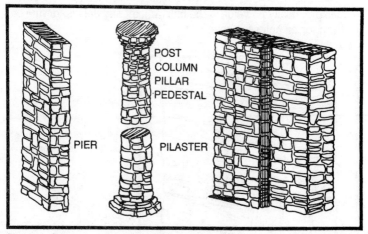

POST
COLUMN
PILLAR
PEDESTAL

PIER   PILASTER

Fig. 9-4. The pier, column and pilaster are important stonework construction parts.

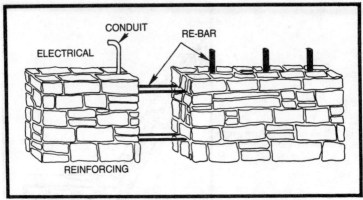

Fig. 9-5. A reinforcing bar, or re-bar, is used when placing conduits.

Dry stone mortar joints will suck the moisture from the tucking mortar and stop it from setting properly. The tucking mortar, is one part waterproof and stainproof cement—white, colored or natural—to 2 to 2½ parts graded sand mixed to a heavy plastic thickness using drinkable water. It should be firmly pressed into the joints in layers until they are full for tooling.

On old work, the joints should be raked out at least to a depth of 1 inch. The joints should be washed out clean and free from loose old mortar. Before troweling the mortar in layers, the joints should be well-wetted with water to kill suction. I find I get a better long-lasting job of tucking by using rich grout mortar for the first layer and following it immediately with the thick or heavy mortar layers.

This layer placing does two things. It helps kill suction. And it leaves practically no voids in the mortar joint and delays, drying out of the mortar before it sets.

Fig. 9-6. A plate anchor is useful in stonework.

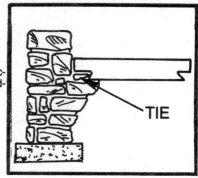

Fig. 9-7. A joist anchor helps accommodate other parts of a building's construction.

TIE

I let the filled mortar joint mortar "take-up" (semi-set) before I tool it (Fig. 9-19). Tooling can then have pressure applied to the joint (Fig. 9-20). The stonework can generally be brushed and cleaned immediately after tooling.

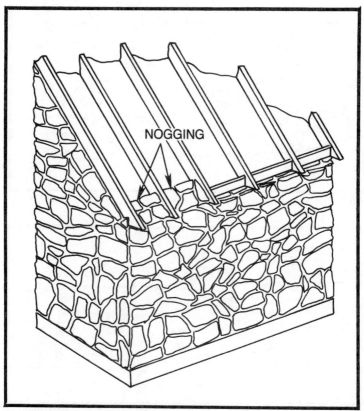

NOGGING

Fig. 9-8. Mortar used for nogging can be fairly weak.

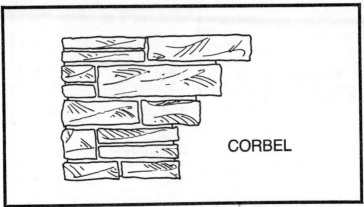

CORBEL

Fig. 9-9. Corbeling is necessary when making chimney tops.

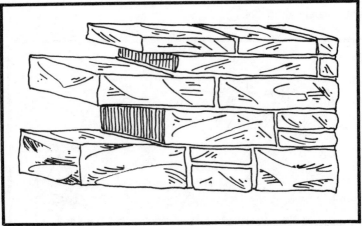

Fig. 9-10. Toothing comes handy when a wall is left that will be continued later.

RAKING

Fig. 9-11. Raking is employed at the corners or leads in stonework setting.

118

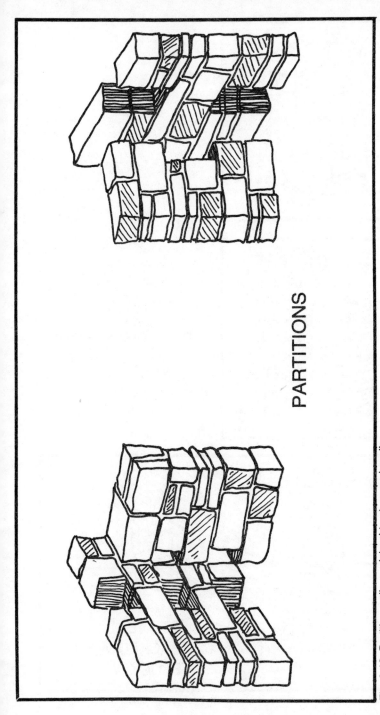

PARTITIONS

Fig. 9-12. Partition walls are joined to stonework walls.

119

Fig. 9-13. Stone backed with block.

Fig. 9-14. Stone backed with brick.

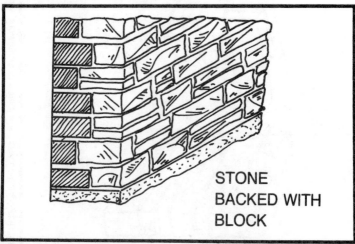

STONE
BACKED WITH
BLOCK

Fig. 9-15. Another example of stonework backed with block.

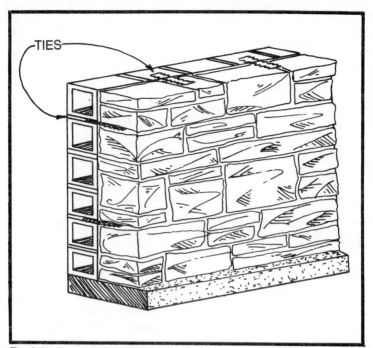

Fig. 9-16. Stonework backed with ties.

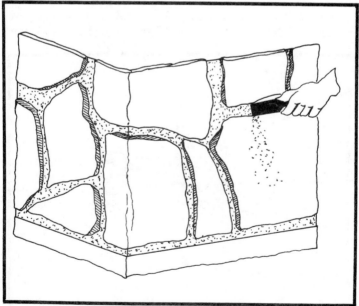

Fig. 9-17. Rake out joints carefully.

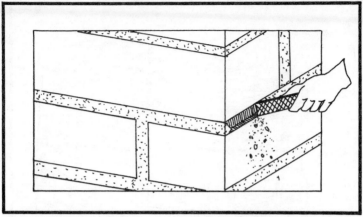

Fig. 9-18. Tucking is performed on new stonework where the mortar joints are raked out or partly filled.

CLEANING

The best cleaning material to use is the old-fashioned lye soap and water. I have used both a steel brush and common scrub brush when washing down stonework. Muriatic acid solution (10 percent to water) is good on stone containing no minerals. Iron oxide in stone will leave a rust-like appearance on the stonework when acid solution is used.

Stone seldom needs replacing. When it does, I always throw semi-thick mortar into the cavity and force the replacement stone

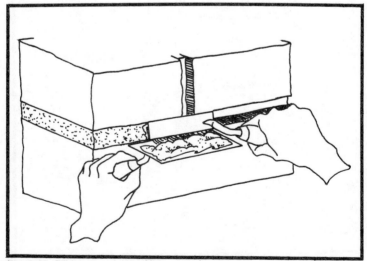

Fig. 9-19. Fill joints and then let the mortar semi-set

Fig. 9-20. Tool the mortar and then clean the stonework.

into the mortar. This way, fewer voids will be left surrounding the new stone.

Tucking and cleaning work should always start at the top of stonework. All cleaning fluids should be well-washed or hosed off within an hour after use. Stonework should not be cleaned with any liquid until the mortar joints are fully set.

Chapter 10
Lintels,
Arches and Walls

The structural purpose of a *lintel* is to span openings and support weight (Fig. 10-1). The *lintel* also holds the opening together as well as apart. It can be of wood, metal, reinforced concrete or other material. All lintels should be at least 4 inches into the wall on each end. Lintels should be of a breadth equal to twice the thickness of the wall. A metal lintel should be strong enough so that it does not sag when the load weight rests on it.

LINTEL SUPPORTS

Some lintels are only strong enough to hold up the weight of a tympanum. They need stronger support above the tympanum to support the weight above. This will require usage of a relieving arch.

Another relieving support is a "Bulls" eye (Figs. 10-2 and 10-3). It is formed like a semicircle arch which is supported by an invert arch. Together they form a circle of stonework, having equal units at the top and bottom and at each side. The *voussoirs* between them reach from the instrados to the extrados. The face distance from the instrados to the extrados shall be at least that of the thickness of the wall.

ARCH CONSTRUCTION

The structural purpose of an *arch* is to span openings to support weight above by resolving vertical pressure into diagonal or horizontal thrust. The face width of an arch should at least equal the

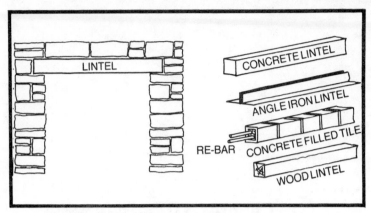

Fig. 10-1. Lintels are designed to support weight.

thickness of the wall it supports. Its depth or thickness should equal the thickness of the wall. An arch may be used as a decorative member or as a structural member within a wall as a blind (Fig. 10-4).

Support or underpinning of some sort is needed on which to set stone when building an arch. A *buck* is best for this purpose (Fig. 10-5). It is held in place by wedges. The buck should not be removed until the arch is completely set. A support such as a lintel and tympanum can be used where it is required.

Arches should conform to the classification of stonework being done unless the arch is for a front display, trim decoration, etc. A rustic style of rubble stonework should have a rustic-appearing arch, unless the arch is set off in appearance by using polished or finely wrought and gauged stone.

The stone in all gauged arches is wrought and sized by sawing, filing, rubbing or using various powered tools. You can also perform

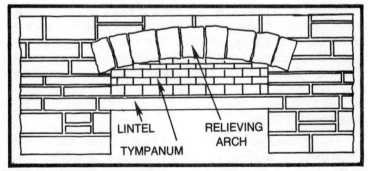

Fig. 10-2. A relieving arch lintel.

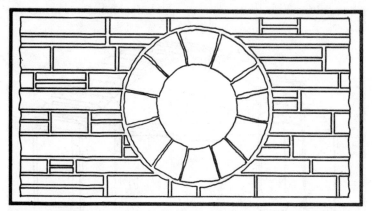

Fig. 10-3. A bull's eye is formed like a semi-circle arch, supported by an invert arch.

chipping with hand tools. Stone is also gauged in stone processing plants and numbered as to size, bevel and where it is to be set in an arch. It will generally require some hand work to fit properly. Gauged stones are closely set in an arch. The joints are even in width and small. The stone is dipped in cement grout or grout having a very fine sand as an aggregate. I always wet the stone with water before dipping to stop suction. The grout should be of the consistency of cream. The stone should be set immediately after dipping. There should never be any voids in mortar joints. This will have to be watched when grout is used, since the moisture is sucked from the grout rather fast unless the stone is well wetted. The slipping of the grout, from a well-wetted stone, is also possible. Should this happen, voids could be in the joints.

Ungauged arches are made with stones that are semi-fit. The joints take up their unevenness of shape. Stiff mortar is used to fill the joints. The longest stone of a key in an arch should always be placed

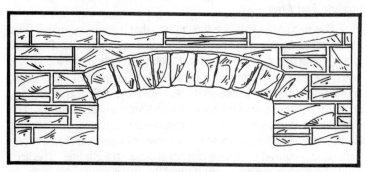

Fig. 10-4. An arch may be used as a decorative or structural member.

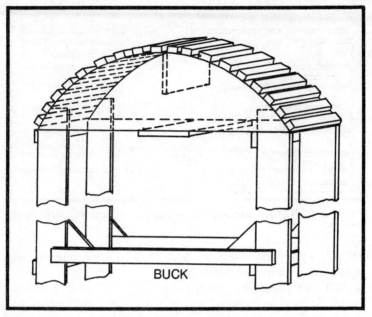

Fig. 10-5. A buck is a support on which to set stone.

at the intrados (soffit, or inside bottom) line of an arch. Where possible, all stones of an ungauged arch should be alternately lapped for strength. This process can be done in gauged arches.

All mortar used in arches should be made with a Portland cement binder. This mortar will better sustain pressure than will lime mortars.

The buck should be held in place with wedges. These wedges can be pulled or knocked out, which makes the buck easy to remove after the arch is set and the mortar is hard.

Straight Flat Arch

The *straight arch* is like the lintel in that it spans openings (Fig. 10-6). It need not extend beyond the opening on its ends. This arch is not as strong as solid reinforced concrete lintels. Welded angle irons, back to back, are sometimes used to strenghten the arch. In appearance, this arch seems to sag in its middle. This sagging appearance can be averted by giving the arch a slight camber. The extrados (top curve of an arch) can be straight and the intrados (bottom line of an arch) can take a camber (slight curve). Or they both can be curved or have a camber from a straight line. The arch will then appear not to sag in its middle.

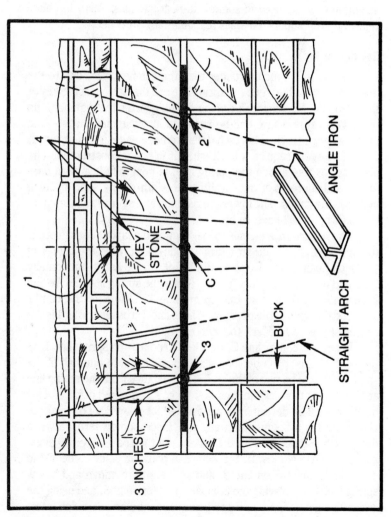

Fig. 10-6. A straight arch spans openings.

Camber Arch

The *camber arch* is a stronger arch than the straight arch (Fig. 10-7). Its strength increases with the more camber it has. It, too, can have an angle iron support. Angle iron should always extend into the jamb at least 4 inches.

Relieving Arch

A *relieving arch* is used in stonework to stengthen lintels (Fig. 10-8). It will carry the weight, should a lintel of wood burn out, become faulty or weaken. The relieving arch is also used as a blind strengthening member in some load-bearing walls. Also, the blind relieving arch supported walls are generally stuccoed.

Segmental Arch

This arch is much stronger than the camber arch, due to the greater distance between the spring line and the bottom of the key at the intrados. This distance can vary. The greater the distance, the more vertical pressure will be resolved into diagonal thrust—and thus a stronger arch. This arch does not need angle iron support. It does, however, require a buck when it is being constructed. The distance, or rise above the spring line, is generally less than one-fourth and more than one-twelfth the width of the span opening between the jambs. The lower the rise, the stronger the abutment at the skewback will have to be.

The *segmental arch* must be laid out on the layout deck in order to have a correctly and structurally sound arch. Find the center of the buck head piece. Refer to Fig. 10-9. Strike line 1 horizontally from end to end of this head piece. This is the spring line. Strike line 2 perpendicularly across this spring line 1. Line 2 is the center between the span of the opening. Where line 2 crosses spring 1 is the center of the arch. Mark this center point C.

From this center line C, on line 1 to point 4 on spring line 1, at the jamb of the span opening, is a distance equal to one-half of the span opening. The rise of the arch is the distance from the spring line at C to the bottom of the arch key on line 2, marked point 3. This distance shall be determined and marked for point 3. (The distance should be for a segmental arch, a distance somewhere between one-fourth and one-twelfth the distance of the span's opening along spring line 1). Now with the compass point at point 4, open the compass to point 3 on line 2, and scribe an arc above and below spring line 1. By placing the compass point at point 3, and using the same distance (from point 4 to point 3), scribe an arc which inter-

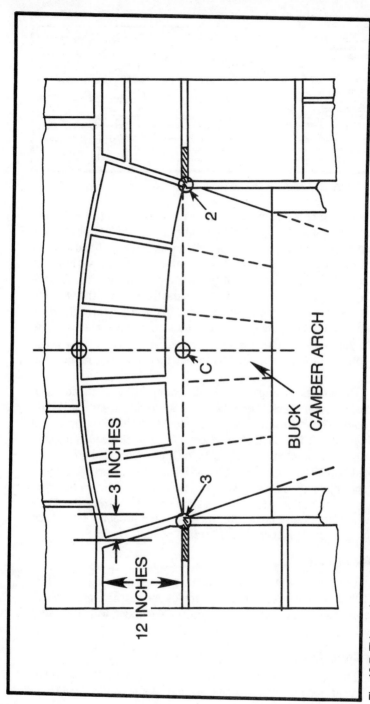

Fig. 10-7. This camber arch is very sturdy.

131

Fig. 10-8. A blind relieving arch strengthens lintels.

sects on the arc at points 6 and 7. By striking a line points 6 and 7, and intersecting line 2, the radial point at 8 is formed. By placing the compass point at 8, opening to point 4, and describing to and through point 3 until the spring line at point 9 is intersected, you will have the intrados of the arch. By extending the compass the width of the face of the earth, at least a distance equal to the thickness of the wall, the extrados of the arch can be scribed. By striking a line through points 8 and 4 and between 8 and 9, and intersecting the extrados of the arch, you will have the correct incline of the skewback lines which are from point 4 to point 10 and from point 9 to point 11, respectively.

The buck head is now marked off. The springer stone width size is marked on the buck. Then the key stone width size is marked on the buck. The width of the voussoirs should now be determined and marked off on the buck. Both faces of the buck head templates should be marked off. Underpinning or frame work and cross slats should be added to the buck head and installed in the proper place in the span opening. Care should be taken to have the buck at the right height for the arch. After the buck is in place, a string should be attached from radial point 8 to the rise, when properly setting the arch stone in alignment with this radial point.

Semicircle Arch

This arch has its radial point C in the center of spring line 1 (Fig. 10-10). From the radial point, the intrados and extrados are scribed. The springer, key and *voussoirs* are in alignment with the radial point.

Low-Crown Arch

The *low-crown arch* is laid out on the buck board. It is placed on the layout deck for marking and shaping. Refer to Fig. 10-11.

Strike line 2 on the center of the buck board (or template) and cross it with horizontal spring line 1. One-fourth the distance of the span opening on the spring line 1 is the height of the arch (3). Open the compass to half the distance of the span opening, that is, from C to 4 on spring line 1. Placing the point at 4, scribe an arc above and below the spring line. Now place the compass point at 3 and scribe an arc intersecting the arc above and below spring line 1 at points 5 and 6. Strike a line through points 5 and 6, and intersecting line 2, to find the radial point 7. By placing the compass point at radial point 7, scribe the intrados, starting from point 4 to point 8. Extending the compass the breadth of the arch face, the extrados can be scribed. In this arch, the springer stones rest on imposts. All the stone members of this arch are aligned with center point C. The skewback inclining slope is not in this arch.

Should the stone members be in alignment with radial point 7, then the springer stone would rest on the skewbacks at points 8 and

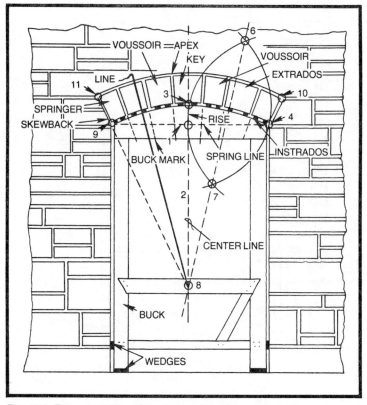

Fig. 10-9. The segmental arch is stronger than the camber arch.

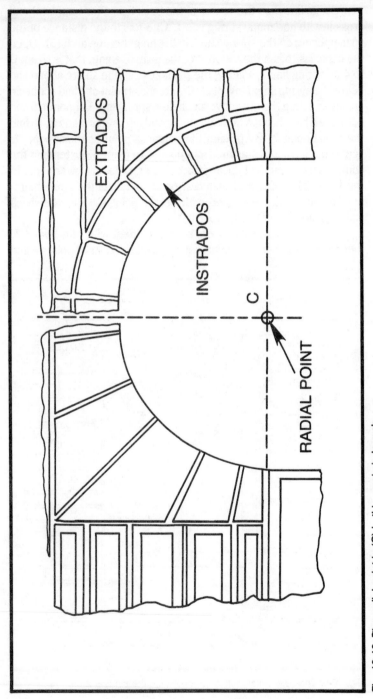

EXTRADOS

INSTRADOS

C

RADIAL POINT

Fig. 10-10. The radial point is (C) in this semi-circle arch.

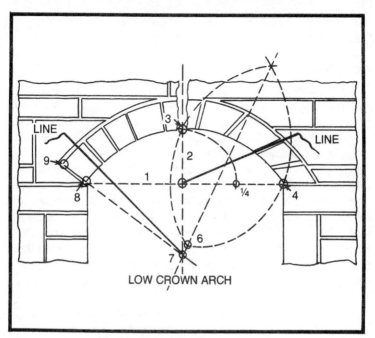

Fig. 10-11. Layout procedure for a low-crown arch.

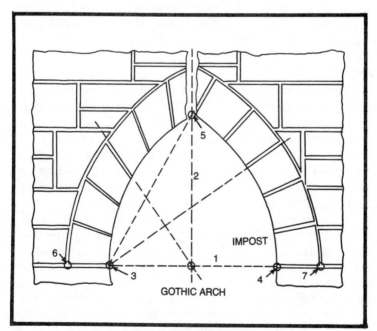

Fig. 10-12. The gothic arch has springer stones resting on imposts.

135

9. The unit widths should be marked off on the buck head template at the intrados.

Gothic Arch

The *gothic* arch is a very strong arch (Fig. 10-12). This arch has its springer stones resting on imposts (horizontal surface) in alignment with spring line 1. Having struck spring line 1 on the buck template, center line 2 of the arch is now struck above and below the spring line perpendicularly through the center of spring line 1. Placing the compass point at 4, and extending it to point 3, the intrados of ½ of the arch can be scribed. By extending the compass from the intrados to the extrados, which is the breadth of the face of the arch desired, the extrados can be scribed. Now place the compass point at point 3, extend the compass to point 4, and scribe the intrados of the other half of the arch. By extending the compass the distance of the face breadth, the extrados can be scribed. This arch has equal distances between points 3 and 4 and point 5 at the bottom of the key of the arch.

The stone members of this arch can align with points C, 3 or 4, and have the springer stones rest on the imposts. Should alignment be at a point from below the spring line, a skewback rest would result for the springer stone. When alignment is made from point C, or a point below the spring line, all the stone members of the arch will be of a different size and shape.

Low-Rise Gothic Arch

This arch, with its low-rise, is used when there is not room for a high-rise gothic arch (Fig. 10-13). On the buck head template, scribe the spring line, and cross it with center arch line 2. Determine the rise at point 3 and the spring line span, opening points 4 to 3. Then from 3, 4 and 5 the arc points 7 and 8 are found below the spring line. In this low-rise gothic arch, the radial point will be below the spring line and not on the center line. This arch is two segmental arches leaned together. Figure 10-14 shows how to find points.

Place the compass point at point 4 to 3 to scribe an arc below and above the spring line. Do the same with the compass point at point 3. Strike a line through the arc points 6 and 7. Then strike a line through points 8 and 9 to find point 8, where this line intersects the radial line struck through points 9 and 8. The intrados and extrados can be scribed with the compass point at point 8 and scribed from point 4 to point 3, then extended for the extrados. The stone members are placed in alignment with points 8, 7, 4 or 5.

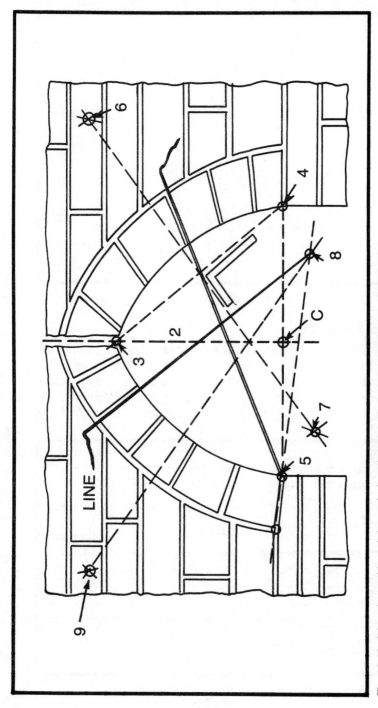

Fig. 10-13. A low-rise gothic arch is used when there is not enough space for a high-rise one.

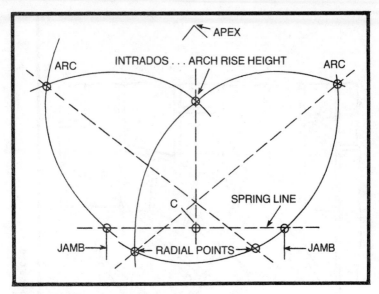

Fig. 10-14. Take time when finding compass points.

Semi-Gothic Arch

This arch has a *semi-gothic* formed extrados and a semicircle arch intrados (Fig. 10-15). It is a very strong and beautiful arch. Its intrados is scribed from point 4 to point 3 to point 5 with the compass point at the radial point C, which is on spring line 1 and the center line 2 at C. After deciding the breadth of the face of the arch at the

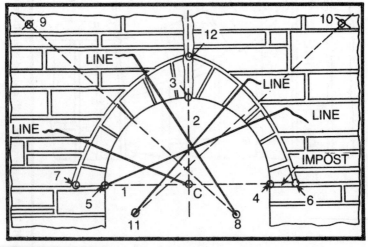

Fig. 10-15. This semi-gothic arch is solid and attractive.

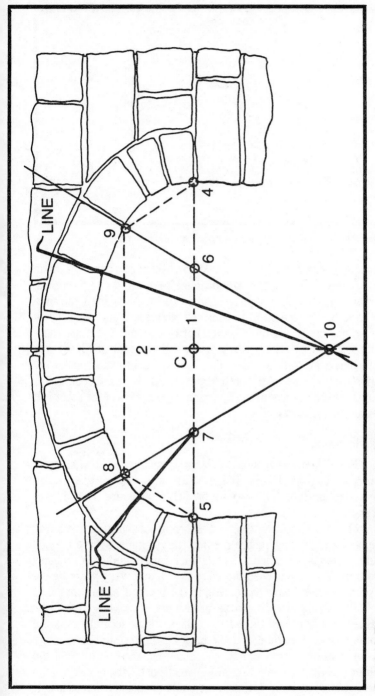

Fig. 10-16. The compass method of laying out an elliptical arch.

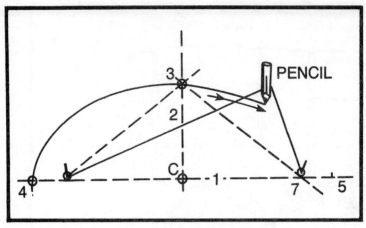

Fig. 10-17. The string method of laying out an elliptical arch.

imposts, points 7 and 6 are found. With the compass point at 7, open the compass the length of the distance between 4 and 5, cut the center line above the spring line and find point 12, which is the apex of the arch. With the compass point at 7, scribe arcs above and below the spring line, using the distance between 4 and 5. Do the same from point 6. Using the same distance, with the point at 12, cut arcs 8, 9, 10 and 11. With the point at 8, having the distance from 8 to 7, scribe the extrados of the arch from 7 to 12. With the point at 11, using the distance from 11 to 6, scribe the extrados of the other half of the arch.

Elliptical Arch

The *elliptical arch* is one of the strongest arches in stonework construction (Fig. 10-16). It springs from springers that set on horizontal imposts. The way its haunch crowns are built gives it strength.

I have used four methods when laying out this arch; the string method, the framing square method, the trammel square method and the compass method. The trammel square method is probably the best. I have not used the compass method very many times, especially when I have had access to the trammel square method.

The string method can be used when a rough arch is to be plastered or stuccoed (Fig. 10-17). It is not as accurate as is the trammeled arch method. Put the buck head template board on the layout deck. Mark off the span opening distance on it. Find the center C of the arch on spring line 1, which connects the jambs of the opening at point 4 and 5. Strike the center rise line 2 across line 1.

From point C, measure up the distance necessary to the required height of the arch desired to point 3. Put the compass on point 3 with the compass extended the distance between point C and point 4. Scribe an arc across the spring line on both sides of point C, and mark them 6 and 7, respectively. Now drive nails at points 3, 6 and 7. Tie a string to the nail at point 6. Pass it around the point 3 nail, and tie it to the point 7 nail. Remove or pull out nail 3 and insert a pencil in the string and scribe the intrados of the elliptical arch. By lengthening the string to a point above point 3, the distance of the breadth face of the arch, the extrados can be scribed with the pencil in the string.

I find the framing square method to be an accurate method if I am careful when I lay it out on the buck board template (Fig. 10-18). Strike the spring line 1, through the span opening distance points at 4 and 5 respectively. Find the center of the span opening on the spring line 1 and designate it point C. Strike the arch rise line through line 1 at point C. Lay the framing square line 1, and the body extending below point C in alignment with the rise line 2.

The trammel rod is a narrow board with a pencil hole at one end or a notch for a pencil. From this notch, A, measure the distance equal to the face breadth of the arch and bore a pencil hole, B, through the rod. From this pencil hole, B, measure a distance equal to the distance from point C to points 4 or 5, and put a pin through the rod at 3B. The distance from 5A to B is the distance equal to the rise of the arch.

Placing the trammel rod on top of the square, the intrados and extrados of the arch can be scribed on the buck board template. I am

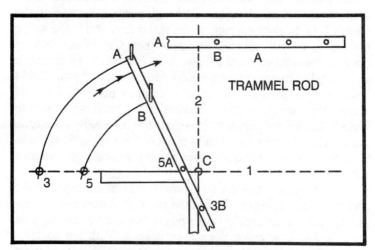

Fig 10-18. The framing square method of laying out an elliptical arch.

141

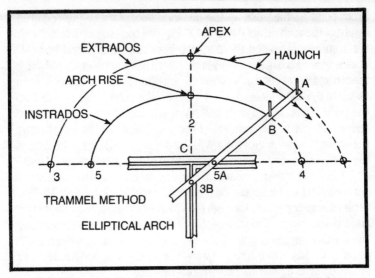

Fig. 10-19. The trammel square method of laying out an elliptical arch.

always careful to keep the pins of the trammel rod tightly to the square as I scribe the arch. The trammel square method is carried out the same way as the square method (Fig. 10-19).

The compass method of scribing the elliptical arch will not make a truly correct elliptical arch. Its appearance is the semblance of an elliptical arch. There are two methods I have used.

With the first compass method, point off the span opening distance on the buck board template and mark them points 4 and 5 respectively. Strike spring line 1 through points 4 and 5. Find the Center C of the span opening on the spring line. Divide the spring line into four equal parts and designate them 6 and 7 each side of point C. Place the compass point at point 7 and scribe an arc above the spring line having the compass opened the distance equal to that from point 7 to point 5. Now place the compass point at point 5 and scribe an arc intersecting the arc scribed from point 7, and having the same distance in the compass. Designate this point 8. By placing the point at point 7, scribe the intrados of the arch from point 5 to point 8. By extending the compass the face breadth distance, the extrados can be described.

Do the same procedure from point 6 and scribe that part of the arch after finding point 9. To find the radial point from the intrados and extrados of the arch between points 8 or point 9, the compass point is placed at either point 8 or point 9. With the compass extended the distance that is between point 8 and point 9, intersect the rise line 2 below spring line 1. Designate this intersect point as 10. Now, with the compass point at point 10, the intrados and extrados of the arch from point 8 can be described to point 9. The semblance of an elliptical arch is now on the template. The stone members of the arch from points 5 to 8 are in alignment with radial point 7. The stone members between points 4 and 9 are in alignment with radial point 6. And the stone members between points 8 and 9 are in alignment with radial point 10.

The second compass method of scribing the semblance of an elliptical arch is more complicated. However, the arch height distance can be designated as described (Fig. 10-20).

Strike spring line 1, the width of the span opening, from point 4 to point 5. Find the center C of the span on spring line 1 and strike the vertical rise line 2, across it at C. Designate the arch height, as required, at point 3 on line 2.

Strike lines from point 3 to points 4 and 5. Take the distance from point C to point 3 in the compass and with the compass point at point C, cut the spring line on either side of point C. Designate the marks as points 6 and 7, respectively. Take the distance from point 4 to 6 in the compass and, with the compass point at point 3, cut the lines from points 4 and 5 to point 3. Designate them as points 8 and 9, respectively. Take the distance from point C to point 7 in the compass. With the compass point at point 4 and point 5, scribe arcs 10, 11, 12 and 13. Where these lines cut spring line 1, designate

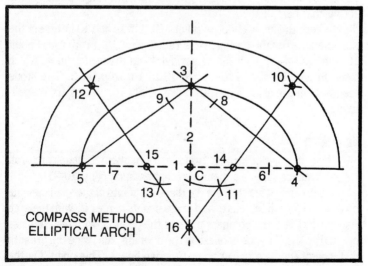

Fig. 10-20. The second compass method of laying out an elliptical arch is more difficult.

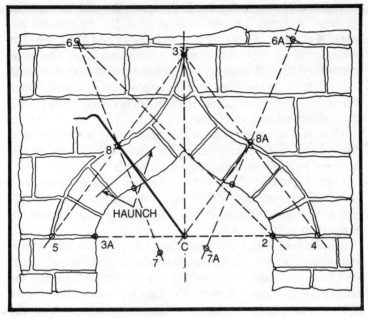

Fig. 10-21. An ogee arch is very decorative.

radial points 14 and 15, respectively. By placing the compass point at radial point 14, the intrados from point 4 to the line from point 10 to 11 can be scribed. This same procedure from radial point 15 will scribe that part of the arch.

Where the struck lines of points 10, 11, 12 and 13 intersect the rise line 2 below the spring line is radial point 16. From radial point 16, the rest of the arch can be scribed from the struck lines, which pass through points 10 to 14 and 12 to 15, to point 3. The stone members are in alignment with radial points 16, 14 and 15, respectively.

Ogee Arch

This arch is not strong. It is more ornamental than structural. Its S-haunches give it a distinctive appearance (Fig. 10-21).

Strike spring line 1, from the distance points of the span opening on the buck board template, and cross it at its center C, with the arch rise line 2. Place the compass point at the point C, with the compass opened up the distance of one-half the opening plus twice the breadth distance of the face of the arch. Cut rise line 2. This point 3 is the apex of the arch. Set back from the jambs of the opening on the springer line, the distance equal to the breadth face of the arch, and designate these points as 4 and 5. Strike a line from point 3 to point 5. Halve this line and designate this point 8. With the compass opened up the distance equal to the distance between point 3 and 8, place the point at point 3 and scribe arcs above the struck line between points 3 and 8. Place the compass, with the same distance, at point 8 and scribe an arc intersecting the arc scribed from point 3. This found point is radial point 6, from which the intrados and extrados can be scribed from point 3 to point 9.

The lower half of this side of the arch is scribed as follows. With the compass point at point 5, and the compass opened a distance equal to the distance between points 8 and 5, scribe an arc below the line struck between points 8 and 5. With the compass point at point 8, and with the same distance, scribe an arc intersecting the arc scribed from point 5. This intersected point is the radial point from which the intrados and extrados of the lower half of this side of the arch is scribed. The other half of this arch is laid out the same way.

Horseshoe Arch

This arch is shaped similar to a horseshoe. It has a tendency to pull out the jamb at the impost (Fig. 10-22).

On the buck board template, strike spring line 1 the width of the span opening from points 4 to 5. Find the center C, and strike the arch

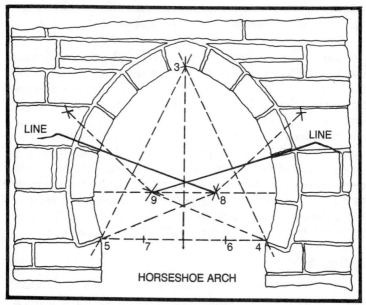

Fig. 10-22. This arch is shaped like a horseshoe.

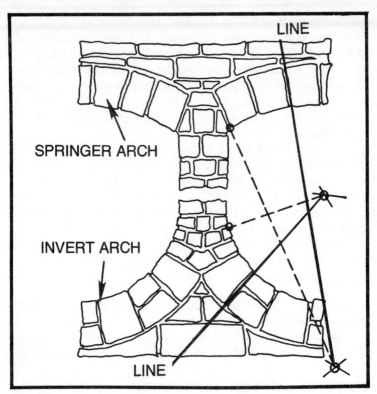

Fig. 10-23. A springer arch can be of different shapes.

rise line 2. With the compass point at point C, having the compass opened the distance equal to the distance from point 4 to point 5, cut the arch rise line 2 and designate it point 3. Divide the spring line from point 4 to point 5 into four equal parts. The point designations shall be 4, 5, 6 and 7.

Now open the compass a distance equal to the distance from point 4 to point 7. Place the compass point at point 4, and scribe arcs on each side of the rise line 2. With the same distance in the compass, place the compass point at point 3 and arc the arcs made from point 4. Designate them 8 and 9. Point 8 is the radial point from which the intrados and extrados are scribed. Carry out the same procedure to complete the other half of the horseshoe arch.

Springer Arch

Springer arches with a spandrel fill are sprung from the same pier (Fig. 10-23). The springer arch can be a semicircle arch, or some of the other arches.

Invert Arch

This is a weight-catching, or distributing, arch. The skewback is at 45 degrees to catch some of the weight.

EGG

An egg-shaped buck template will be useful when constructing an egg (Fig. 10-24). Strike an extended spring line 1, and strike the extended rise line 2, at right angles to it. Take one-half the distance of the spring line 1, from 3 to 4 in the compass. With the compass point at point C, scribe the intrados above the spring line from point 3 to point 4. Now, open the compass a distance equal to the distance of the spring line from point 3 to 4. With the compass point at point C, arc cut the extended spring line 2 and find the radial points 5 and 6. Place the compass point at point C, with it opened equal to the distance between points 3 and 4. Arc cut the extended rise line 2, below spring line 1. Designate this intersection as point 7. Now scribe this rise line 2 into four equal parts from point C to point 7, and

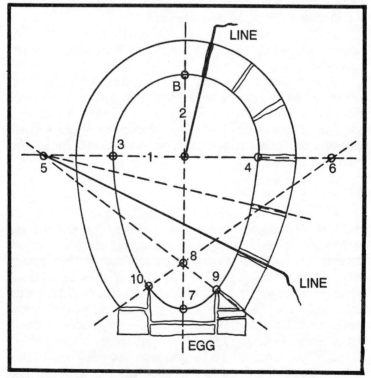

Fig. 10-24. Use an egg-shaped buck template to construct an egg.

Fig. 10-25. Walls are popular masonry projects.

find the radial point 8. Strike a line from point 5 and point 6 through point 8.

By placing the compass point at the radial point 8, the intrados can be scribed from point 7 to the lines struck from points 5 and 6. When placing the compass point at radial point 5 and 6, the intrados from 3 and 4 can be scribed to the lines struck through point 8. Thus, the egg layout on the buck board template is completed. The egg has been used for sewers.

WALLS

Various types of walls are pictured in Figs. 10-25 through 10-29. Stone garden walls are generally low as are property-dividing stone walls. However, some stone walls are high enough to support some sort of roof, such as a patio or car port shelter. Many garden walls do not have mortar, in which case many spalls are used, as chinking is necessary to keep the stone units somewhat horizontal and in place. The best stone walls are those which have cement mortar used for setting the stone. The mortar can be left as is, raked out or tooled. Generally, I use a whisk broom and brush the filled joints, or just brush the joints crossways and call it good. This brushing takes place just after the mortar takes its initial set. The stonework is less likely to get messy then.

Fig. 10-26. This wall is not particularly difficult to build.

Fig. 10-27. This wall features different sized and shaped stones.

149

Fig. 10-28. An attractive looking wall.

Fig. 10-29. This wall has been constructed carefully.

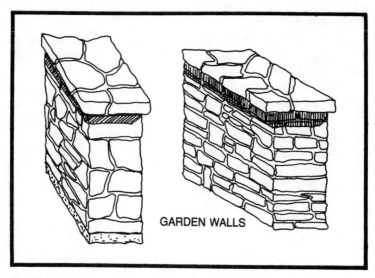

Fig. 10-30. Garden walls are usually made with fieldstone.

Garden Walls

Garden walls are generally made with fieldstone as cobble stonework when mortar is used (Fig. 10-30). Stratified stone is used in rubble stonework walls. Sometimes rustic ashlar stonework walls are made. In this stonework, where long stratified stone is procured, lookout holes can be left in the garden wall. This method of laying a garden wall gives a pleasing appearance. All garden walls are generally capped with coping.

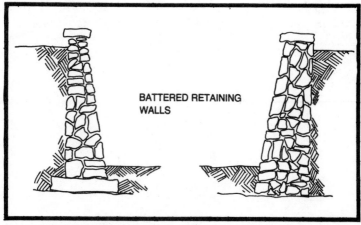

Fig. 10-31. A retaining wall should be battered toward the wall it is to retain.

Retaining Walls

A *retaining wall* should be battered (slanted) toward the wall it is to retain (Fig. 10-31). Cement mortar should be used in this kind of wall, as it will have to contend with moisture.

When a retaining wall is used to hold back an enormous pressure weight, the footing should have concrete posts extending down, sometimes as much as 6 feet into the ground. This will help keep the battered wall from tipping out due to the pressure.

These retaining walls stay longer when they have re-bars reinforcing, both horizontal and perpendicular, in them. Retaining walls are capped with coping.

Chapter 11
Stone Paving

Flat stratified stone, shale stone, shale and even split cobblestone are used for long-lasting walkways, and patios, either indoors or outdoors. Irregular-shaped stone and matched or unmatched wrought stone also are used for street and road paving. They have sustained the heavy traffic of cars, trucks and buses. However, concrete and asphalt paving are taking the place of stone on highways.

Artificial stone, as well as stone inlayed in concrete slabs and blocks, are set like stone. Stone can be scattered about and seated in the ground as stepping stones. They shift about and settle unevenly and are subject to frost. They need resetting at times.

Where an excavation is done, and gravel and sand are packed as a bed to set the stone on, the stones generally stay put. Grass can be planted between them in the dirt-filled joints. The grass needs cutting through the summer.

Where excavation is performed, and concrete is poured on a gravel bed, stone can be set in the concrete. The stone will not shift about or settle unevenly. Such a job on stonework will keep an even and level plane.

Where stone is set in mortar and mortar slushed in the joints, the stone will stay put if it has a void-free bed joint and vertical joint. Where there are voids in mortar joints, condensation of water will collect. Should this water freeze, cracks will form in the joints due to frost upheaval.

153

Stone used in a walkway or patio may vary in size, depending on the method and kind of work performed and walkway or patio required. Walkways and patios that have the stone put right on the ground without excavation would have an uneven surface unless all the stone used were of the same thickness. It is very uncommon if stone can be found of the same thickness.

Where stones vary in thickness it is best to tamp the thicker stone down with a tamper. A walkway and patio should have an even surface plane. This tamping may require the dirt below the stone to be soaked with water in order to seat the stone. This surface leveling can be done by using a straight edged 2 × 4 or 2 × 6-inch lumber at least 4 feet long

Dirt can be put in the joints after the leveling. Grass seed can be scattered along the joints. If the joints are large enough grass, sod can be cut and tamped in them. The joints could be filled with sand or gravel. The bottom of the joint is salted to keep grass in the joints.

This kind of walkway and patio will generally require the stone to be leveled and tamped to place from time to time. Should there be good drainage from this walkway or patio, the leveling will be done less often.

WALKWAY AND PATIO CONSTRUCTION

When a *walkway* or *patio* is built on a tamped gravel and sand bed having good drainage, the stone used should be as near the same thickness as possible. This will require less tamping and straight edge work.

The sand and gravel mix used as a bed for the stone should be well tamped. If a mix of sand and gravel that will tamp to a solid base cannot be found in or near the walkway or patio location, the best way to hold it in secure place is to scatter a dry lime and Portland cement mix over the tamped gravel and sand base. Then sprinkle the base with water. When this mixture of gravel, sand, lime and cement sets or settles together, it will stay put. The stone put on a mix of this kind and seated to an even plane will generally stay in place a long time. It will not need resetting very soon.

The joints can be close or even 4 inches apart. Close joints should be flushed with a grout cement mortar. A scrub brush should be used to work the grout into the joints. A wide joint can be filled with gravel, sand, dirt or sod.

When the excavation for a walkway or patio is filled with tamped gravel, sand and concrete is poured on to a thickness of less than 6 inches. This concrete should be reinforced with welded wire.

Stone can be seated and tamped to a uniform even plane with the help of a straight edge. The joints should be filled with concrete, if large joints, or with a cement mortar if the joints are small. Should they be close, it is best to use a cement grout mortar.

When stones are set in mortar, whether on gravel and sand base or a concrete base, the joints should be filled with mortar. A straight edge should be used to seat the stone to an even level plane.

When stone is placed on a wood floor or decking as a walkway or patio, the procedure is as follows. Secure stone for this job that does not vary in thickness over ½-inch and that holds uniform throughout the stone. Cover the floor with tar paper, felt or simply tar or coat the floor with a good waterproof sealer. Should the floor get wet, it will likely swell and crack or upheave the stonework. Cover this paper or coating with welded wire. This reinforcing will help keep the stonework from cracking at the joints.

The best way to fill joints with mortar is to thoroughly wet the joint after they are cleaned out. Loose material should not be left in the cleaned joints. Mortar should be put in the joints and packed with jointer tools. A layer of mortar should be put in the joint at a time. The following layers should be added and packed before the previous layer is semi-set or dry. Always be sure that the place where the mortar is put should be damp with moisture (water). The joint can either be struck and tooled with a jointer or just brushed crossways of the joint with a whisk broom, scrub brush, metal brush or just plain gunny sacking.

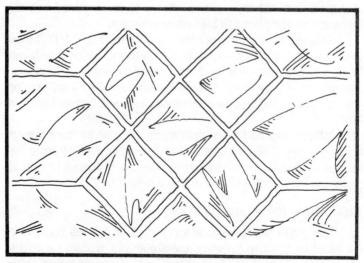

Fig. 11-1. This star patterned stone walkway is very unique.

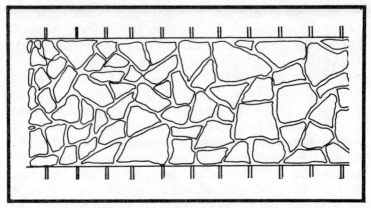
Fig. 11-2. This stone walkway has a brick border.

After the walkway or patio stonework is set, it should be swept and washed down with strong lye soap. An acid mix, 10 to 15 percent; muratic acid to water, may bring out the mineral in the stone and leave it appearing rusty. This is a good way to make stonework look old.

Mortar used for walkways, patios, etc., should be made with waterproof cement—one part cement to 2½ to three parts good graded sand. The joints can be tooled or brushed and kept damp with water to keep them from drying out before they are fully set, or at least well set initially. The joints can be covered with sand or sacking that is kept wet until the joint mortar is set. I give all outdoor stonework for walkways, patios, etc., a slight slope and be sure there are no low places to hold water on them.

Stonework walkways can have a pattern (Fig. 11-1). Stone used in patterned walkways or patios, whether inside or outside can be sawed, tool pitched or used just in their natural form, size, etc. The one major thing to watch when choosing stone for a walkway or patio is thickness of the stone. However, a smooth surfaced stone is best.

Patterns can be formed with stone and also by the different colors of stone. The best long lasting stonework should have stone that are as near the same strength as possible. The grain texture of stone will help to choose stone of like lasting quality.

EXCAVATION, FORMS AND PATTERNS

This patterned stonework walkway is of cobweb bond. It is bordered by brick which gives the stonework walkway a unique appearance (Fig. 11-2). These stones used were hammer-pitched.

Herringbone Pattern

The herringbone pattern is generally a hard pattern to keep in alignment (Fig. 11-3). A straight edge should be used as well as a line for the purpose of keeping the stone on an even plane. This pattern requires that the stone be uniform in size as well as of a somewhat uniform thickness. This stone can be shaped to a uniform size with hand tools or a saw. Stones can, with care, be broken or chewed off to size by using a stone cutter.

Excavating Tips

Excavating for a walkway should have a slightly slanted, packed bed for drainage purposes. Perforated drain pipe or a ditch may have to be used to protect the walkway from holding excess water under the stonework. The water may freeze and upheave the stone.

Figure 11-4 depicts the different parts of this walkway. Note the drain tile. This tile should drain off water to a lower altitude or to a perforated drain tile field.

There are many bond patterns of stonework in walkways, patios, etc. Figure 11-5 shows the way the edging border stone is seated. It can be seated in dirt, mortar, or concrete, depending on the kind of walkway or patio that is made.

Cobblestone Walkway

A cobblestone walkway is easy to build as the stone does not need wroughting (Fig. 11-6). When choosing this stone it is almost necessary to have the stones uniform in size, at least in diameter.

Border Patterned Walkway

Figure 11-7 depicts a cobblestone walkway bordered by broad flat strata stone. This stone patterned brickwork can be of different kinds. However, it is best to set all the stone, including the border

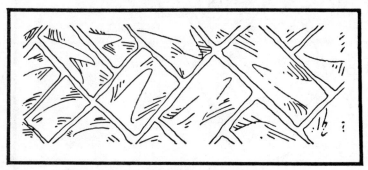

Fig. 11-3. A stone walkway with a herringbone pattern.

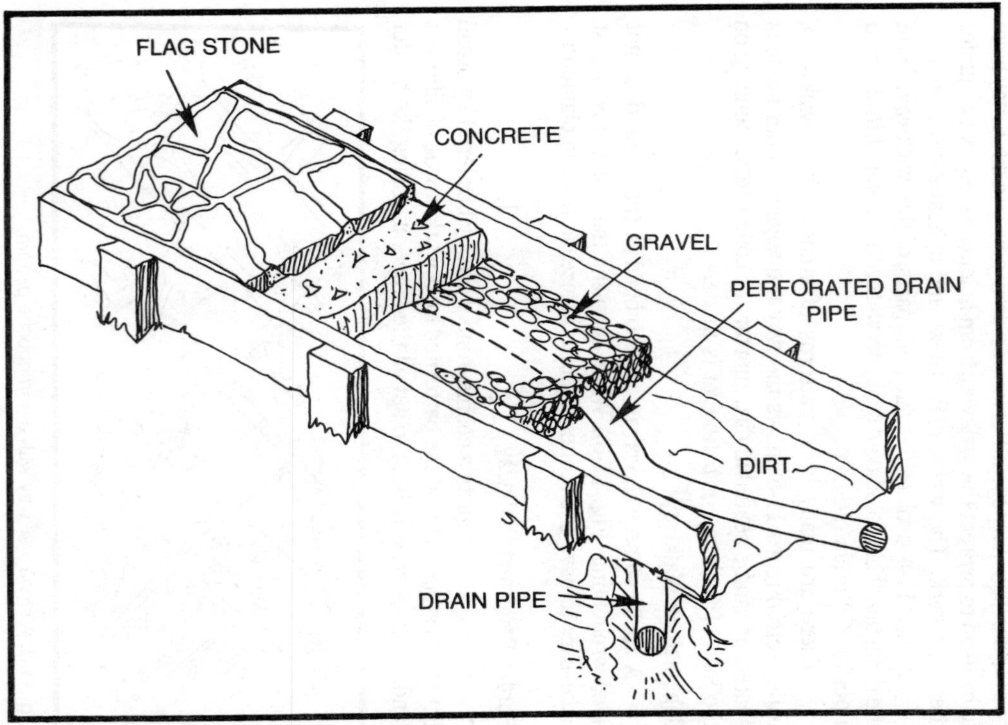

FLAG STONE

CONCRETE

GRAVEL

PERFORATED DRAIN PIPE

DIRT

DRAIN PIPE

Fig. 11-4. Take time when doing excavating.

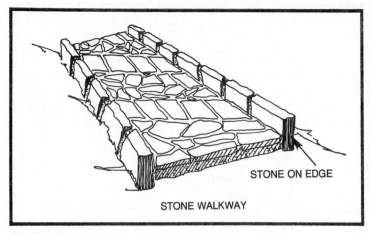

Fig. 11-5. Border stone is seated in dirt, mortar and concrete.

stone, in a fresh concrete pour. Figure 11-8 depicts excavating and leveling procedures.

Running Forms

The stakes or re-bars should be driven in the ground and brought to grade by the use of a level. Excavation should be deep enough to allow for sand or gravel, plus concrete and stone where they are required. Preferably, forms should be lower on one side for drainage.

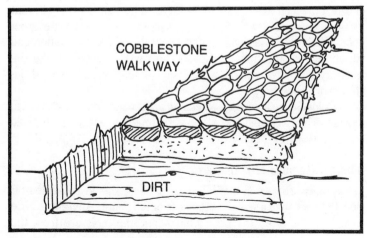

Fig. 11-6. A cobble stone walkway is not difficult to build.

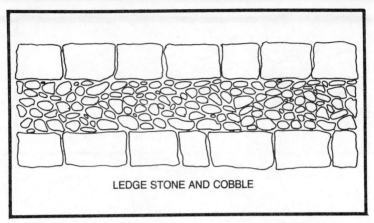

LEDGE STONE AND COBBLE

Fig. 11-7. This cobble stone walkway is bordered by broad, flat stone.

Forms are sometimes run before excavation but generally after excavations. Forms should be straight and have the same required shape as each other. The form on the lower side should drop approximately ⅛-inch to 4 feet to give drainage to the finished stonework.

The forms should be well staked to stay in place. Braces are sometimes required (Fig. 11-9). The top of the forms should be free from stakes in order to run the screed on them during the pouring and stone setting.

Inside Walkway Parts

Inside stonework on a concrete slab or deck should have a bed of sand on which to set the stone. Figure 11-10 shows the different parts of this inside walkway. This walkway sets on a waterproof floor. The parts used will let the concrete be free in motion and vibration from the house proper. The parts stipulated make the walkway a secure part of the building. Reinforcing helps hold the stonework together.

Welded 6-inch wire mesh can be used when the stone is set in mortar. This will hold the stonework together and help to avoid cracking (Fig. 11-11).

Different Methods of Walkways

Stonework set on a wood floor or deck should be sealed off from the floor with a sealer on the floor or felt paper. Anything can be used that will keep the floor from taking the moisture from the

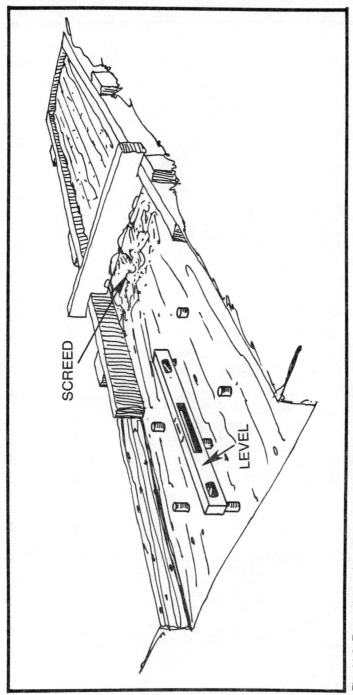

SCREED

LEVEL

Fig. 11-8. Excavating and leveling are important construction processes.

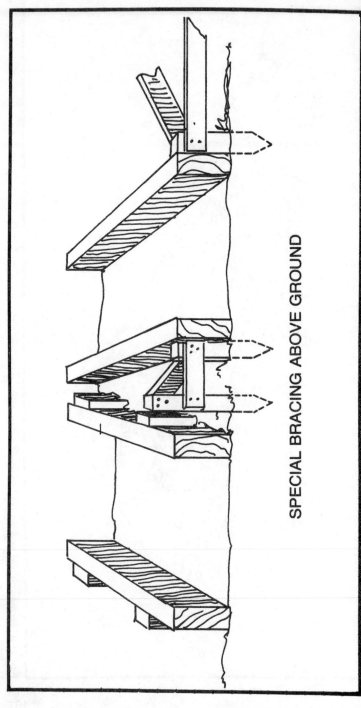

SPECIAL BRACING ABOVE GROUND

Fig. 11-9. Braces keep forms in place.

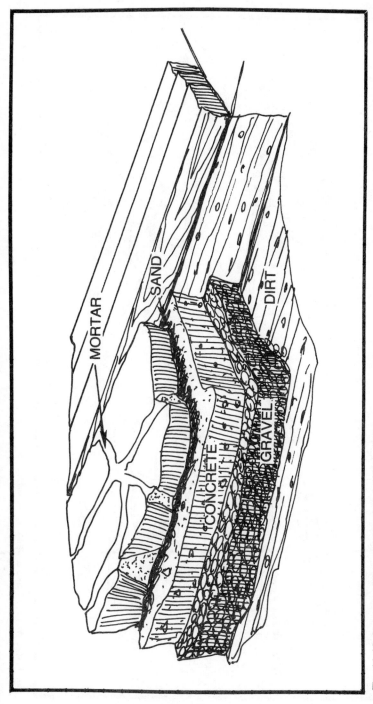

Fig. 11-10. Here are different parts of an inside walkway.

163

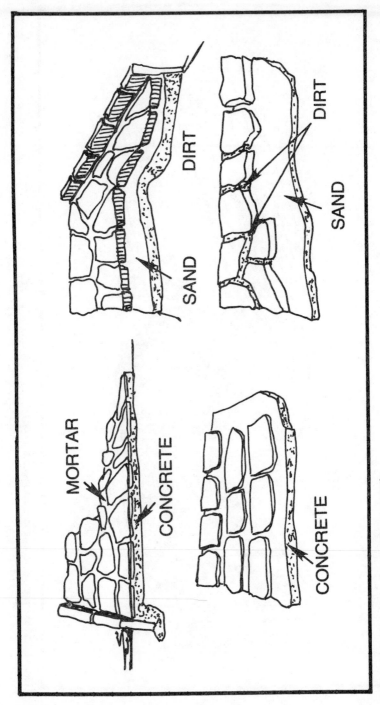

Fig. 11-12. Ways to make a walkway or patio.

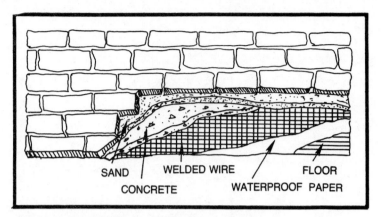

SAND   WELDED WIRE   FLOOR

CONCRETE   WATERPROOF PAPER

Fig. 11-11. Use welded wire to help prevent cracking.

stonework. Wood flooring will swell with moisture and may crack the stonework.

In Figure 11-12 are some methods of making a walkway or patio. It depends on where a walkway or patio is to be put as to which method should be used in its construction. The stone will also in some cases dictate the method to be used.

Chapter 12
Steps and Planters

When building stone steps, stone should be set in waterproof cement mortar. If set on a concrete slab, the stone shoud be set when the concrete is semi-set and the concrete should be well-wetted with water and grouted with neat cement (cement and water mixed to a thin cream consistency). This method will insure the best results and eliminate most voids in the stonework. The joints should be tooled with pressure, brushed crossways and tooled again, then well-brushed when firmly set or semi-cured. The joints should be kept damp for a few days and not allowed to dry out until set. Cleaning solutions may be used, but old-fashioned lye soap and a good scrub brush is the best. A muriatic acid solution will cause mineral rust when used on some stone for cleaning purposes.

REINFORCING STEPS

These steps are reinforced with bars, both crossways and lengthways (Fig. 12-1). The bars should be not over 12 inches apart. They can touch each other where they cross. This makes a network of reinforcing. Use ⅜-inch bars for small steps and larger bars for bigger and longer steps. Steps should be on a good solid foundation and footing. They should be well-secured to the foundation of the house. Steps should not be perfectly flat or level. The steps should have a slope equal to a ⅛-inch drop to a 4-foot run.

The stones used in these steps were sawed to size by a diamond blade saw. Steps can be of almost any kind of stone. The stone used should have a nearly flat surface. This makes the best stone to walk on.

Many stone steps have been built with cobblestone and concrete. I find that these steps last longer than cobblestone set in mortar. I suppose this is due to the cobblestones being round or near round. Reinforcing will help hold cobblestone steps together even though the cobblestone is set in mortar.

STONE TRIM

Stone trim on a business building or a home gives a distinction to the building. Any of the stone bonds and kinds of stone can be used. Any form of setting and various depths of colored mortar can be employed. There are, however, some things to consider when choosing the various kinds of stone. The factors include the kind of building the stone trim goes on, the color of the mortar and the kind of mortar joint appropriate for the stone, bond, and method or form of setting the stone.

Trim on a business building should be the kind that will draw trade or take the eye, so to speak, and give the patron a feeling of security when dealing with those in the business building. Stone used should be master handled, cut and set. It should be stone that looks as though it took considerable labor in its wroughting and setting. The stone and even the workmanship of this stonework should seem to show something extra from the customary built stonework.

Dressed stone should be used in a business building. An ashlar style or bond is more aristocratic. Color, texture and kind of stone is important in stonework on this kind of building. Even the joints should be tooled with exceptional care. Colored mortar should not clash with the color of the stone. The mortar should blend somewhat with the stone used.

The stonework should be clean from mortar droppings and should not be disfigured by the mortar color. Joints should be all of the same width. The stone finish of each stone should be like that of the other stone. Since the joints are kept the same distance from the marginal line, the mortar will appear flat, neat and finished.

Decorative panels of stonework put on business buildings should not be used on a house. The trim on a house can be varied as to size, texture and color of the stone used. However, the same color of stone, method of setting stone, tooling of the joints and stone bond used should be carried throughout the stone trim on a house.

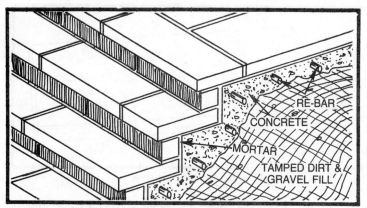

Fig. 12-1. These wrought stone steps are reinforced with bars.

The amount of stone trim on each house will have to be considered and governed by the kind of house the owners desire. In all trim stonework, architectural proportions will have to be considered. Trim stonework on a house should give a beautiful pleasing appearance and enhance the value of a house.

Steps can be placed, and the method utilized can result in both a beautiful and useful addition to a house. However made, the pattern stone and joints should all coincide with the trim on the house.

A flower box (planter) of the stone should also coincide with the stonework of the house (Fig. 12-2). The size, location and height of the planter should be in proportion with the house proper.

The patio and walkways may vary some but not to the point that any part of them will clash with the stonework on the house. If done

Fig. 12-2. This house is enhanced by the stone veneer trim, planter and stone steps.

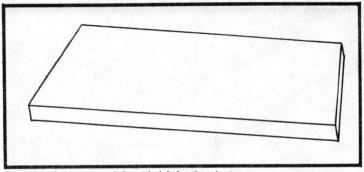

Fig. 12-3. A concrete reinforced slab for the planter.

properly, this house will be architecturally correct and pleasing to the eye.

PLANTER CONSTRUCTION

Planters are made in various shapes and sizes. They require a drain. The planter slab should be set on a good foundation that has a good footing (Figs. 12-3 and 12-4).

Figure 12-5 shows the cross section of a planter. Flashing is required when a planter is made next to a wall. Water should not get between the planter and wall.

A planter can be made with stone on a concrete or other backing. A thickness of 8 inches is best for the walls. Sloped walls

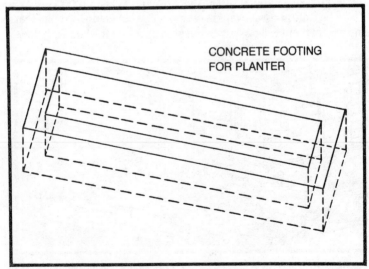

CONCRETE FOOTING
FOR PLANTER

Fig. 12-4. The planter needs a concrete footing.

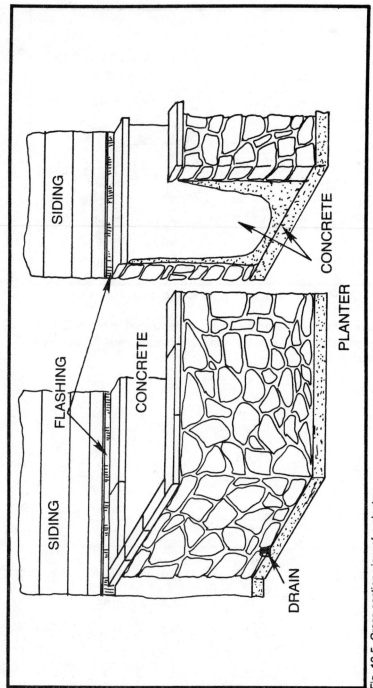

Fig. 12-5. Cross-section view of a planter.

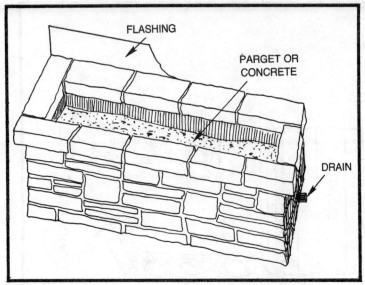

Fig. 12-6. A sawed stone planter. Make sure you allow for a drain.

and a cupped bottom on the inside of a planter will let frozen dirt rise instead of pushing out the walls. Allowance must be made for drainage (Fig. 12-6).

Chapter 13
Fireplaces

The different parts of a fireplace have certain names. Figure 13-1A is a manufactured fireplace unit of which there are other makes on the market. Figure 13-1B is an ash door and Fig. 13-1C is an ash dump. Figure 13-1D is a damper (one brand that opens or is hinged on the bottom). An angle iron is used above the firebox opening as a lintel (Fig. 13-1E). Figure 13-1F is a galvanized tie and Fig. 13-16 is a bar used for reinforcing.

CHIMNEY

A *flue* or *chimney* is generally called a chimney *stack* (Fig. 13-2). It carries out smoke from a fire. Cold air traverses down a flue and is returned at the smoke table. It takes out the smoke with it.

Flue Liner

A flue liner, whether square, oval, round or rectangular, is used in a chimney stack. Pargeting is also used: however, in many localities the zoning laws require a flue liner.

To cut a hole in a clay flue liner it is necessary to fill the liner with sand (Fig. 13-3). This will help insure the liner from cracking when it is worked on. It is also best to use this sand filling when cutting a liner in two.

A well-constructed chimney stack will take out the smoke. During this process, the flue will create a strong suction as the air

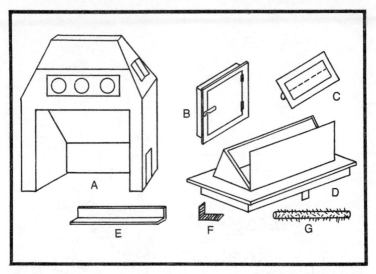

Fig. 13-1. (A) is a manufactured fireplace unit. (B) is an ash door. (C) is an ash dump. (D) is a damper. (E) is an angle iron which is used as a lintel. (F) is a galvanized tie. (G) is a reinforcing bar.

goes down a flue of a chimney stack and returns with the smoke. The smoke shelf should be below any damper or smoke inlet vent or the down-draft of air may, and most likely will, go into a firebox and smoke up a room.

Chimney stacks in zoning areas require a flue liner. This liner should extend 10 inches below the smoke intake opening. In some cases, where there is more than one smoke intake opening, the smoke may seep into the one not in use. When insulation in a home or room is such that all air is shut out, the air to operate a fireplace or other unit in use may come down the flue of a chimney stack and fill the room or house with poisonous smoke. More than one person has suffocated in this manner. A fire requires oxygen to burn and may not go out even if this air has to come from the flue it is using. All units should have a means of receiving air to safely operate. A chimney stack should extend at least 3 feet above any roof or object which is, horizontally, within 10 feet of it.

There are many types of chimney tops (Fig. 13-4). A chimney stack top that has a flue liner sticking up high may draw out smoke the best. It cannot be controlled, however. A chimney stack with a tile liner extending far enough not to be over an inch above a sloping cap is one that can be controlled. A convexed cap will stop its drawing to some extent, whereas a concave cap will increase its drawing. I generally make a straight cap.

174

The chimney stack size is governed by the fireplace opening size to the firebox hearth. The height of a chimney stack is governed by this very thing and by zoning regulations. Where there are large

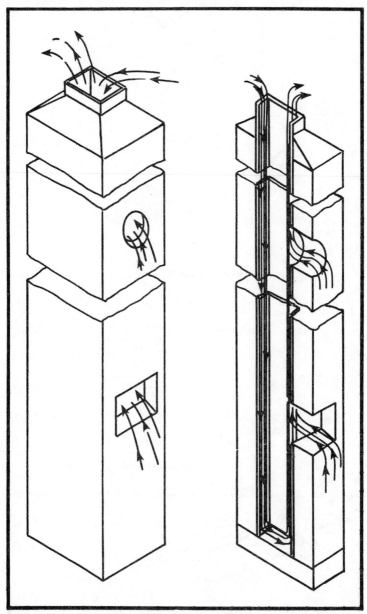

Fig. 13-2. Air circulation pattern in a chimney stack.

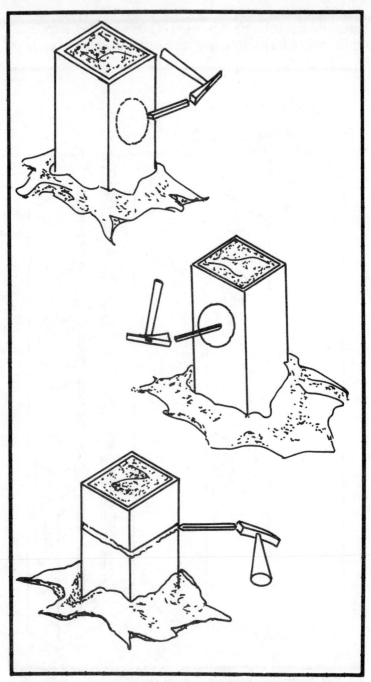

Fig. 13-3. Fill the liner with sand to keep it from cracking while you cut a hole in it.

amounts of snow or rain, a chimney stack may require a cap (Fig. 13-5).

Chimney Flashing

Chimney stack tops require *flashing* to keep water from entering a building. Chimney stacks should not be fastened to any struc-

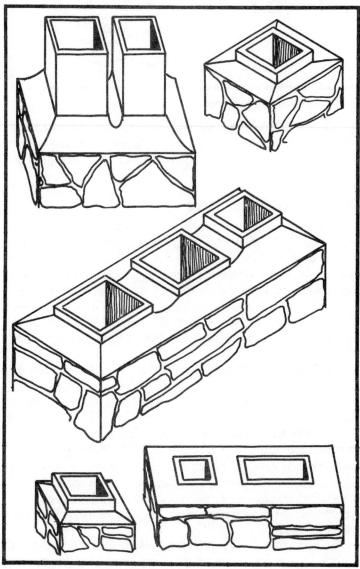

Fig. 13-4. Various types of chimney tops.

Fig. 13-5. Chimney stacks may need caps.

ture. Clearance should be at least 1 ½ inches to give the stacks free motion and allow them to settle evenly. Fastening a chimney other than with flashing may cause it to have cracks in its stonework (Fig. 13-6).

FIREPLACE SUPPLIES AND TYPES

There was a time when only rock and mortar were needed to build a fireplace. Today we have things like dampers, ash dumps, ash cleanout doors and formed metal units which have in their walls places for circulation to throw out heat. Angle irons, re-bars and fans to circulate air through cavities in units are important devices.

The angle iron should be long enough to extend into the stonework at least 4 inches at its ends. It should have freedom to expand from heat. This can be accomplished by placing insulation at its ends.

Ash dumps should not be difficult to open. Ashes must be allowed to fall into the ash pit. The clean-out door should close completely tight to keep out drafts. It should be no smaller than 8 by 8 inches.

Dampers are differently made. Some damper blades hinge in the middle and others hinge on the side. Some are flat with equally raised sides and ends and others are raised on one side only. I like the ones that have damper blades hinged on the side and are higher on the side opposite the hinge. They should be large enough to accommodate the fireplace size in order to amply handle the smoke of the firebox fire.

Re-bars come in different sizes and are used throughout a fireplace to help hold it together. Liners should be of a size to accomodate the smoke of a fireplace fire according to the damper size of the firebox, the throat and the fireplace opening. Fireplace units generally take care of the fireplace firebox, the throat and the damper.

Fireplaces can be built one on top of the other, or one on each floor above the other. These are stacked fireplaces. The method of carrying out the smoke stacks, chimneys and ash pipes is shown in Fig. 13-7.

Back-to-back fireplaces are generally built where there is a partition to have a fireplace in each room. One footing holds both fireplaces (Fig. 13-8).

FIREPLACE PROPORTIONS

All the parts of a fireplace interior should be of a size that will make them all work together for the best operation. The parts are in proportion to the fireplace opening. The height of the opening can be determined by the height of the chimney stack required. If the chimney stack is 24 feet high, an opening may be raised 1 inch. Should a chimney stack be 16 feet in height, the opening could possibly be lowered 1 inch. The width of the opening can equal its height. A 24-inch opening height with a 24-inch width opening is suitable for a 20-foot high chimney stack. A fireplace opening can be less in height and width than just stated but never more (assuming the chimney stack is 20 feet high).

The flue liner area should be at least 12 percent of the opening area. This can vary with the chimney stack height. Should the chimney stack be 26 feet high from the hearth, the flue area can be reduced to 11 percent of the opening area. If the chimney stack is 14 feet high, the flue area should be 13 percent of the opening area.

The firebox (inside hearth) depth should not be less than two-thirds the width of the opening measure. The back width of the

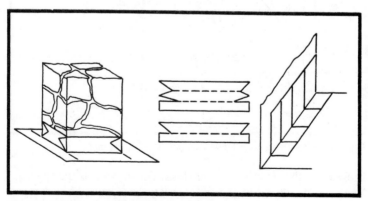

Fig. 13-6. Flashing keeps water from entering.

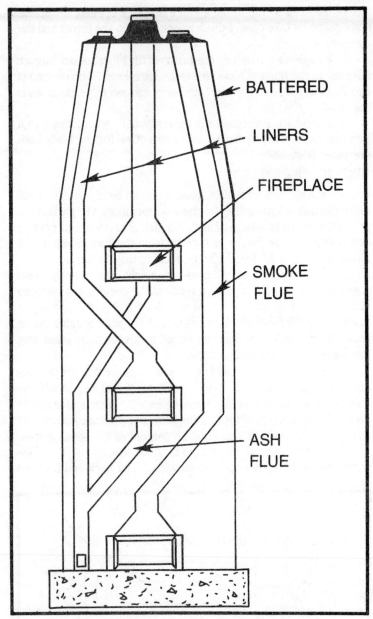

BATTERED

LINERS

FIREPLACE

SMOKE
FLUE

ASH
FLUE

Fig. 13-7. Stacked fireplaces are built one on top of the other.

firebox hearth should be one-third less than the width of the opening. The height of the opening should not allow the slope in the back of the fireplace firebox to be more than 40 degrees from vertical.

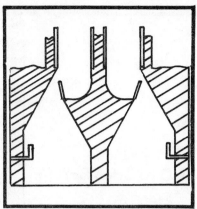

Fig. 13-8. A back-to-back fireplace.

The damper opening should be at least long enough to cover in width the throat of the fireplace. This will not block off the smoke that enters the smoke chamber. The throat area should be one-half to two-thirds of the liner area. The sides of the fireplace firebox should never slope more than 30 degrees from vertical. The distance from height of the throat should be at least one-third the height of the opening. The damper plate should not open beyond 1 inch to the vertical inside of the liner. A smoke shelf should be below the bottom of the damper frame for best results. It can be much, much lower. Liners should not rest on any fireplace unit that may be used. In fact, any unit, even the damper, should be free to expand and have no weight or pressure on it. The fireplace could crack, as many of them have, when this is not watched in construction. There are seven kinds of units in use and, if installed properly, make for a good fireplace.

All chimney stacks should be at least 3 feet above a 10-foot horizontal point to anything that may be there. Zoning laws have, in many places, regulations governing fireplace construction. The fireplace stacks and walls should be at least 8 inches thick on all outside stonework. This helps lessen condensation in a flue, which will require less repair and upkeep.

If, during the building of a fireplace, you build the face of the fireplace separately to the fireplace below the mantel, the face can be taken off and changed. Ties should be used to hold this face to the fireplace (Fig. 13-9).

FIREPLACE CONSTRUCTION

A fireplace that smokes from anyplace except out of its top chimney stack is dirty and expensive to use, as smoke damage and

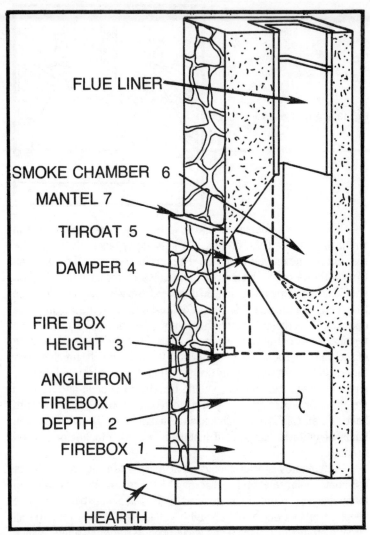

FLUE LINER

SMOKE CHAMBER 6

MANTEL 7

THROAT 5

DAMPER 4

FIRE BOX HEIGHT 3

ANGLEIRON

FIREBOX DEPTH 2

FIREBOX 1

HEARTH

Fig. 13-9. A guide to fireplace construction.

repair is costly. A fireplace must be reinforced, as is its footing, to keep from cracking or coming apart enough to smoke in the wrong places, making it inoperative. Faulty construction has ruined many fireplaces.

Fireplace Footing

The first thing you should do when contemplating construction of a fireplace is to check out the location to see if it is feasible. Can a

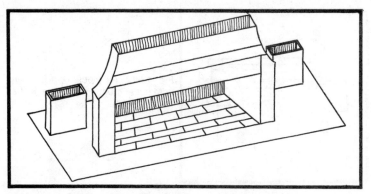

Fig. 13-10. A fireplace on a slab should be reinforced with bars.

good footing be put there? It is better not to build unless you can put a solid footing there to build on. Fireplaces made with stone are heavy. The footing has to be put below frost level and not on soft soil. A well-tamped gravel bed is of use when pouring a footing with concrete or setting stone for a footing. Footings should extend at least 8 to 10 inches beyond the fireplace proper on a good underbed much more on medium underbed. They should not extend at all on poor underbed as the fireplace may settle, possibly unevenly, and crack.

A fireplace slab should be cross reinforced with bars. It should be at least 4 inches thick (Fig. 13-10).

Fireplace Foundation

The foundation should be reinforced and not be put on a green or unset footing. Any work on a fireplace should not be done when the mortar or pouring might freeze, as freezing will ruin the material. Some fireplaces are set right on a deep thick footing with no foundation required. Then again, a low-reinforced foundation is needed on which to set a basement fireplace. Many fireplaces are set, one on

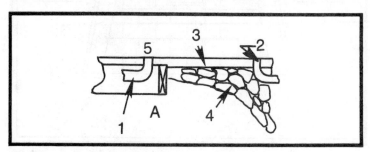

Fig. 13-11. A trimmer arch holds the fireplace hearth.

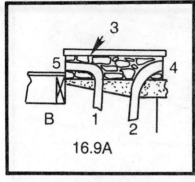

Fig. 13-12. Air pipes for a fire can vent out at the top front or back of a raised hearth.

the other, in which case a trimmer arch or a concrete slab is used to carry the hearth of the main floor fireplace.

Trimmer Arch

A fireplace *trimmer arch* is used to hold the hearth (Fig. 13-11). An air pipe can come from outside and extend through the hearth next to the fireplace opening. It supplies oxygen for the fire.

A trimmer arch can also be a reinforced concrete slab. Air pipes can be used in either kind of trimmer arch. They can vent out for the fire either at the top front of a raised hearth or at the back, as well as through the top of the hearth (Fig. 13-12).

Fireplace Layout

I have built many fireplaces that do not smoke up a house or structure. It is best to lay out the positions of fireplaces and flues for the chimneys or pipes below in the basements, etc (Fig. 13-13).

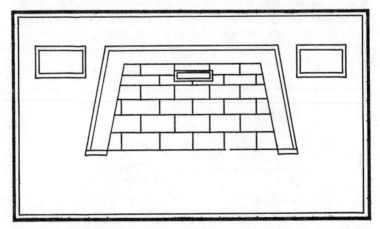

Fig. 13-13. Do the fireplace layout carefully.

184

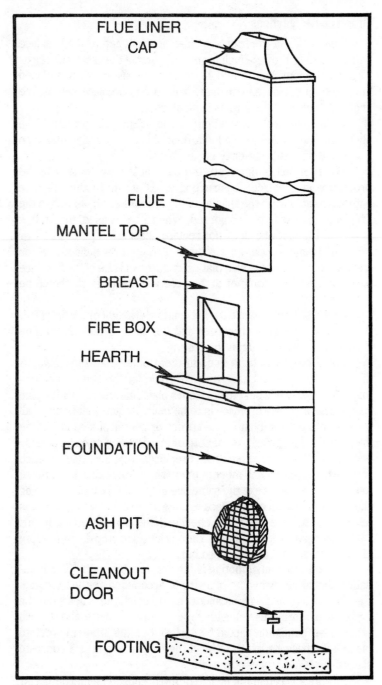

FLUE LINER
CAP

FLUE

MANTEL TOP

BREAST

FIRE BOX

HEARTH

FOUNDATION

ASH PIT

CLEANOUT
DOOR

FOOTING

Fig. 13-14. Some parts of a fireplace.

Fireplace Designations

The wings on the fireplace sides are fastened to the fireplace with ties unless they are built in and are a part of the fireplace breast. The ash cleanout door in Fig. 13-14 is in the basement. It is placed low, next to the basement door. Where one fireplace sets above another, both could use this cleanout door.

If the ashes are cleaned out of the ashpit, this pit should be above ground level. The cleanout door should be on the outside so ashes and dust will not dirty up the house.

Where a unit is not used, the plan must vary some, and the procedure in fireplace construction is different. In the fireplace without a unit, care in the shaping of the firebox hearth, as well as the fireplace box, has to be considered. When a unit is used, the firebox is part of the unit and does not require shaping.

The hearth should be strong to hold up its weight as well as traffic loads. A concrete slab that extends the full size of the fireplace is best. However, trimmer arches are also used. Both should be well-reinforced.

Re-bars should extend the full length and height of the fireplace. A bar should be at each corner and between, if necessary. The corner bars should start in the footing.

Some fireplaces have flues in them other than their own. A fireplace plan then will have to make room for the flues. The flues may vary in size. It is best to draw out a plan. Make sure that the plan can fit wherever the fireplace is to be built. Requirements may call for a fireplace to be built in the corner or center of a room. Some fireplaces should be across, next to or in a partition or on an outside wall. Then, too, I have built four fireplaces together, one for each room where four rooms meet in the corner. More than once these four fireplaces had use of the same flue in the chimney stack. Zoning requirements require a fireplace to have its own flue. However, it is permissible to have more than one flue in the chimney stack. In this case, you must have the flues at various levels to stop down-drafting of the smoke from one to the other.

A good substantial footing is always a requirement. The foundation should be always be of a size to accommodate the fireplace. The foundation, in many instances, has to catch the ashes from the fireplace or fireplaces, should there be one or more above each other. The foundation should be corbeled on the inside in order to make a flat base on which to build the fireplace, unless a concrete slab or large flat stones are used.

Firebrick is laid in the hearth of the firebox. The mortar is just fireclay and water mixed to a cream-like consistency. Bricks are dipped in the mortar and set tightly to each other. Allowance has to be made for the ash dump, should one be required. The firebrick can be flushed with mortar after they are laid. When this mortar dries, it can be wiped off with sacking. The ash dump flange can be set on or recessed in them.

Where a unit is used, it can be set on the slab or can be set on the firebrick. I generally set it on the slab and cut the firebrick to fit. Using this method, the firebrick are easier to replace when they need replacing.

Units should be insulated with fireproof material for expansion. The insulation should be as nearly fireproof as is possible. Stonework should not touch the unit. The unit should not have anything resting on it. It is necessary that the unit be completely free to expand when heated. The flue must not set on the unit. There generally are directions with respect to the unit from the factory. Hot and cold air openings in the unit can open on the front or sides as desired.

The stonework in a fireplace should be reinforced from the footings to the top of the chimney stack. It should also be reinforced every 2 feet around to hold it together, according to some zoning regulations. I have built many fireplaces without as much reinforcing. I wrought the stone needed and used a good mortar mix.

A good mortar mix for a stone fireplace is one part Portland cement with ¼ part lime to three parts good sharp graded sand, mixed with drinkable water to a stiff mix. Color can be included; but not over 10 percent to the binder.

When there is no unit, the firebox will have to be shaped. I use firebrick when shaping the firebox and throat. The damper is set on the stonework and kept free so it can expand when heated. You can

Fig. 13-15. These fireplaces have openings on one side.

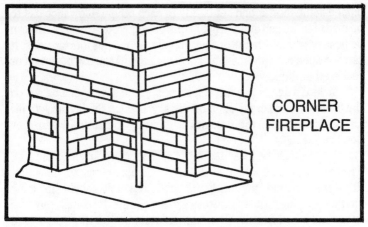

CORNER
FIREPLACE

Fig. 13-16. A corner fireplace can open on the side and end.

shape the smoke chamber above the damper with firebrick. These brick are smoother than stone. It is best to leave the firebrick free from the stonework, as the heat in the firebox will cause the firebrick to expand.

The fireplaces in Fig. 13-15 have the openings on only one side. The hearth does not extend to the width of the fireplace breast. It does extend the required zoning distance from the firebox.

Corner and Open-End Fireplaces

A corner fireplace that opens on the side and on the end needs a good stout corner steel post on which to hold the angle iron that carries the stonework above. The damper is above the firebox (Fig. 13-16).

A fireplace with openings on the opposite sides can have the damper above the openings or on the bulkier side of the fireplace (Fig. 13-17).

Where a fireplace opens on the sides and the end, two posts are required. If the firebox has a slab top, the smoke is carried out through an end damper (Fig. 13-18).

If a fireplace opens on the sides, as well as the end, and the stonework is carried up above the firebox, the damper can be above the firebox or at the end opposite the end opening. The posts will have to be stronger in this fireplace (Fig. 13-19).

Barbeque and Outdoor Fireplaces

There are many kinds and sizes of barbeques and outdoor fireplaces. Some are just thrown together, even without mortar, and

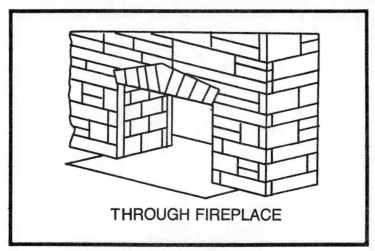

THROUGH FIREPLACE

Fig. 13-17. This fireplace has openings on opposite sides.

others are quite elaborate and finished in the proper way. There are combinations of barbeque and fireplace outdoor stonework that are built with care.

I am always careful when building an outdoor fireplace or barbeque to have the chimney stack of a large enough size to take care

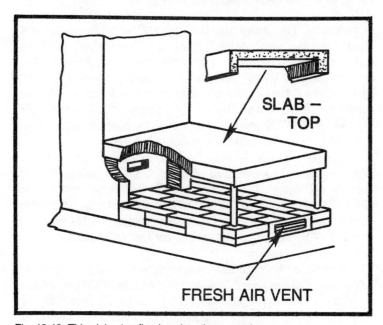

SLAB —
TOP

FRESH AIR VENT

Fig. 13-18. This slab - top fireplace has three openings.

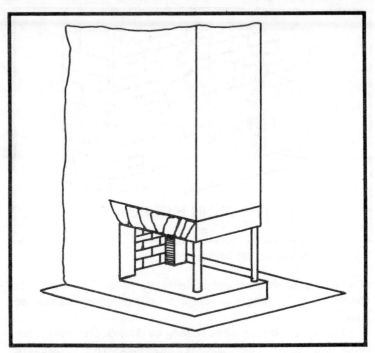

Fig. 13-19. Another fireplace with three openings.

of the smoke. The smoke table is always well below the smoke vent place. I put the vent openings apart, not together and with one higher than the other. The largest one is always lower than the others. The vent should never be over one-eighth the size of the liner. Where there is more than one vent, the combination's size should not be larger than five-eighths the size of the chimney flue.

In Fig. 13-20 the smoke is sucked into the liner through vents in the liner. The smoke table is well below the vents.

The barbeque and outdoor fireplaces having grills, grates, Dutch ovens and combinations of these should be built to fit such units-as necessary. These units are on the market and can be obtained in various sizes. The fire grates can generally be adjusted to accomodate the kind of fire used. A dome screen should be used to contain half-burned paper and sparks that roar out of outdoor chimney stacks on occasion.

Barbeques built outside will burn wood, coal or charcoal briquettes. Coke is generally used when a barbeque has an oven.

This outside barbeque has a grill unit and a fireplace built in it (Fig. 13-21). The fireplace has a metal top on which cooking can be carried on when the fireplace is operating. Wood, coal or charcoal

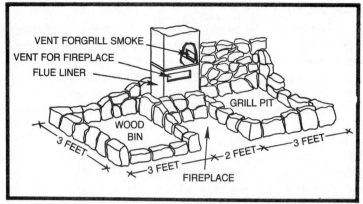

Fig. 13-20. One type of barbeque and fireplace combination layout.

can be burned in the grill unit as the inside grate can be raised for coke or lowered for wood or coal.

The outdoor barbecue shown in Fig. 13-22 has an interesting layout. There is a grill in one wing of the barbeque. On the other, there is arranged an electric spit. It can burn whatever fuel desired. The center fireplace is made to use wood as fuel. In this barbeque there is not a metal top for cooking above the fireplace. There is a need for two side vents and a middle vent in the lines to carry out the smoke.

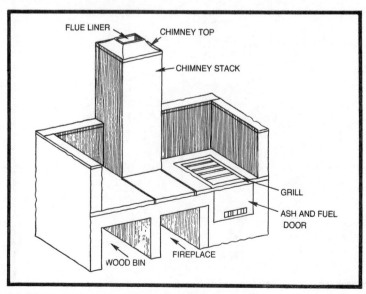

Fig. 13-21. This barbeque has both a grill and a fireplace.

BARBEQUE PIT

One kind of barbeque pit is complete with patio and places to sit (Fig. 13-23). It can all be placed right on the dirt and using a larger joint between the patio stone, will let grass fill the joints. However, it is best to have the seats of stonework placed on concrete footing. I prefer a concrete slab to set everything on except the firepit.

The firepit should be excavated to a depth of 1½ to 2 feet deep. It should have gravel (75 percent round 2 to 3-inch pebbles) fill up to where the fire will be. The pebbles will, when heated by the fire on it, hold the heat. The size of the pit should be no larger than is necessary for the number of people using it. Seats should be close enough to the pit that you can reach it when roasting morsels at the end of a rod, willow, etc. Don't place the seats so close that you

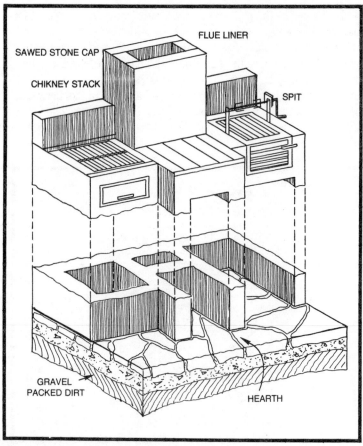

Fig. 13-22. A barbeque, fireplace, grill and spit combination.

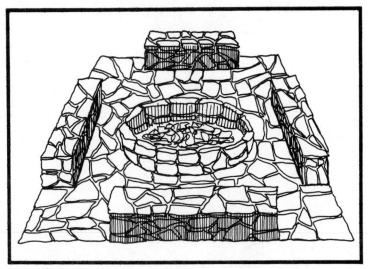

Fig. 13-23. An open pit barbeque like this one is ideal for cookouts.

become hot and have to stand behind the seats. A temporary grill can be placed on all or part of the firepit, if desired.

This outdoor open firepit is a dandy for cooking marshmallows, weiners and even fish or steak on holders or willow branches. Wood, coal or coke can be burned in this firepit. Smoke should not be too much a problem as there are stone seats around the firepit.

Chapter 14
Aquariums
and Stone Bridges

When building an *aquarium*, the first thing to consider is what size to make and where to locate it. Then determine the kind of stone needed or required to build it. Figure 14-1 shows an aquarium that is made with ashlar stone.

BUILDING THE AQUARIUM

This ashlar stone comes in various sizes, widths and lengths. The depth of this stone varied from 3 to 4½ inches. Its length was from 8 inches to 5 feet 2 inches long. The stone had to be sized as to its depth for this job. This sizing was required for the purpose of plastering on the inside of the aquarium after the stone was laid.

The quantity of travertine ashlar stone to make this aquarium was ordered. It required 56 square feet of stone face for this job. The stone varied in width from 2 to 10 inches, including one joint. There were less of the 10-inch size than the smaller joints.

The pattern of this bond of stone setting was two stones to one. The back of this aquarium had the larger stone. While the front had the smaller widths. The sizes were mixed in size from 2 to 10-inch breadth stone.

The face of this ashlar stone was rustic. The arris was true and even. Most of the natural face protruded beyond the arris. Each stone was cut for depth size to be exactly 3 inches, which required all the ashlar stone to be separately measured and cut on the diamond blade saw for the same depth size. This process took considerable time.

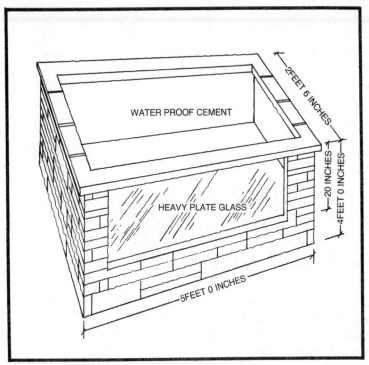

Fig. 14-1. This aquarium will make fish happy.

The lengths of this stone were cut during the setting as required. These lengths varied. When cutting for the required lengths, care was needed as this travertine stone is a brittle stone. It is easily broken. A hammer should be used for this cutting. The corners should be lightly struck with the blade of this hammer. After all the arris corners are grooved by the hammer, a sharp blow with the hammer's square face to the side of this stone between the groove corner cuts will break it. The end arrises will extend from cut groove corner to corner and many not require pitching. Should this stone break when the corner is grooved, pitching will be required.

The mortar could be with or without color. The cement binder can be Portland or white water-resistant cement. Water-resistant cement is not required as the inside of the aquarium is plastered with a waterproof mortar. The inside is also painted with a waterproof sealer.

The glass used in this aquarium is ¼ inch in thickness. It is installed from the inside and sealed to keep water from leaking out at its edges. A back is required in the glass opening to leave a set back shoulder for the glass to set against.

The bottom of the aquarium water tank is made by pouring a concrete slab. This slab is reinforced with ⅜-inch re-bars laid cross ways near the bottom of the concrete slab. The stonework is reinforced with ¼-inch pencil steel. This aquarium can have a metal tank installed in it. When this is done, the inside of the aquarium will not require plastering.

MAKING THE STONE BRIDGE

The stone bridge in Fig. 14-2 is made with fieldstone, and laid up with a cement mortar, 1 part Portland cement to 3 parts graded sand. It is reinforced with ½-inch re-bars. Two bars were used in the top and at the bottom of the sides. The deck or bottom of the bridge (walkway) was reinforced with ¾-inch re-bars installed about 2 inches from the bottom of the concrete pour. The concrete slab was 4 inches thick. These re-bars were placed lengthways and cross-ways about 10 inches apart.

Stone used for the walkway was seated in the concrete just before it took its initial set. The joints were filled in after all the stone was set. No stone used was less than 2 inches thick nor more than 2½ inches thick in the walkway.

Forms were used to get the curvature of this stone bridge. The sides were of stone and not veneer or concrete. Fieldstone was split and pitched. It was set in a cobweb bond, as was the walkway.

The mortar joints of the walkway stonework were filled in with a cement mortar. Just after its initial set, it was cut off and the loose mortar was swept off the stonework. The joints were then brushed

Fig. 14-2. A stone bridge makes a beautiful addition to your property.

crossways with a whisk broom and left to set up. The stonework joints of the sides, both inside and outside, were raked out and filled with a black color mortar. The joints were tooled with a ½-inch convex jointer which left a good joint projection, resulting in a nice appearing convex joint.

The aprons (sidewalks) were concrete. This bridge sat on a stonework foundation that had a concrete footing with a gravel base. Stone was used from the footing to the bridge.

Chapter 15
Stone House

A house can be built of stone (Fig. 15-1). It can be laid up with one kind of stone or a combination of several kinds of stone. The stone used should be of as near a uniform strength and hardness as possible. It should have the ability to withstand nature's elements.

The mortar should be the same throughout the stonework for an equal length of life throughout any particular kind of stone construction. The foundation of a stone house should be placed on either solid rock, gravel, or on as near hardpan clay soil as possible. The ground should not absorb moisture readily or shift or settle unevenly.

Stone houses have been and are built on almost every kind of landscape, even slapped on the side of a hill or atop a cliff. However, it is best to pick a location for a stone house on soil that will stay put and not shift or settle. Stone houses are heavy and do require solid material on which to set. Wide footings will to a great extent offset the faults of semi-firm soil on which to set a house.

PRELIMINARY PROCEDURES

The first thing you have to do when contemplating building a stone house is to have or secure the money for its construction. The location and size come next. Construction in many locales will have to conform to zoning regulations as well as all health and safety requirements. If you do not build the house yourself, you will need a contractor or workmen to do the construction for you. All things thus

Fig. 15-1. This completed stone house should last a long time.

far taken care of, you next need an architect to draw up the plan of the house within its allowable zoning size. Or you do this yourself. A typical house is shown in Fig. 15-2.

After these preliminaries are taken care of, the necessary materials for construction will need consideration. Materials should be obtained and placed on the building location after the necessary excavation is done. During excavation ample room is required. Building materials would generally be in the way should they be placed on the building site.

HOUSE LAYOUT

The layout of the house should be within the bounds of zoning backset and sideset regulations. Some zone requirements also stipulate the height of the house. It is best to have a surveyor locate the front and side marginal lines of any structure to be built, especially when the building is in zoned settings.

After surveying, the batten boards should be put in place, preferably back from the house corners at least 4 feet (Fig. 15-3). The house should be squared.

The corner stakes should be set back from the house layout stakes at least 1 foot. The excavating can now be done without disturbing the setback stakes or the batten boards. After excavation, the proper corners should again be located.

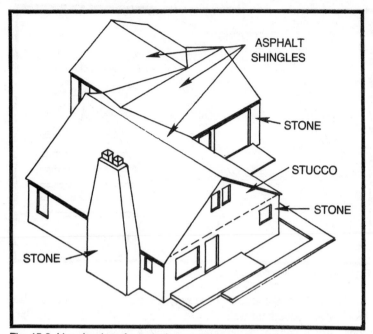

Fig. 15-2. Line drawing of a typical stone house.

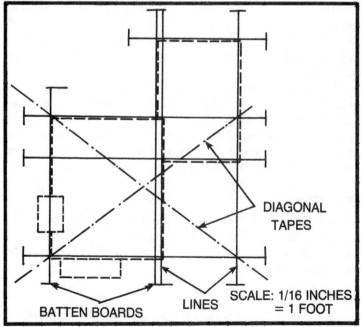

Fig. 15-3. Layout plan for a stone house.

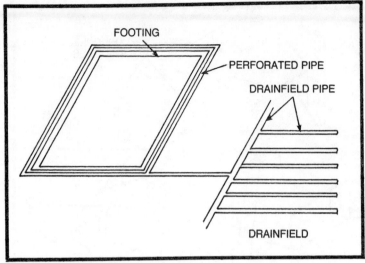

Fig. 15-4. A drainage field may be needed.

Should a basement be required, the necessary forms for the footings and basement walls should now be installed. However, this house under consideration does not have a basement.

The depth of any excavation should not be deeper than that required for the footing. Should the depth be deeper than that required, gravel should be put in to the required depth. The gravel should be well packed. Every 3-inch thick layer of gravel should be well tamped. The gravel should pack well and not swell with absorption of moisture.

When there is a chance of water getting at the footing, there should be some way for it to drain off. Circling the outside of the footing of the house with perforated tile or loose gravel or rock will let the water seep off. These drain methods should have a drain outlet to take off the water to a lower altitude. If there is no lower altitude, then a drain field may be required (Fig. 15-4).

EXCAVATION

The depth of the excavation of this house is to the gravel. It is possible to have a uniform depth distance from the level horizontal lines of the batten board layout. The footing and foundation are poured together.

FOOTING

The footing is poured up to an equal distance from the horizontal level guide lines (Fig. 15-5). The concrete footing and foundation walls are poured together. Stakes of ⅜-inch re-bars (the necessary length) are driven into the footing excavation to a horizontal level distance from their top to the guide lines. The concrete is poured to the top of these stakes. Stakes can be left in the concrete or taken out. The stakes for the house in Fig. 15-2 are taken out. They are put approximately 4 feet apart. It is necessary to put forms above ground level to the required height, which is to the main floor plate on which the joists are put.

The concrete mix is 1 part cement to 5 parts good, graded gravel. (The aggregate is 2 parts graded sand to 3 parts good, clean gravel). The poured footing has two ⅜-inch reinforcing bars embedded in it.

When a concrete wall is poured on the footing, it should be horizontally level at its top. It should be wide enough to accommodate the necessary stone wall and the subfloor it is to carry. Anchor bolts or re-bars may be required to anchor the wall. For the house in Fig. 15-2, the concrete wall is poured only to the bottom of the floor joist plates, which are above ground level the required distance from the first floor level (benchmark). Forms are used above ground. Since the footing and the foundation walls are poured together, the footing and walls are the same thickness. No forms are used below the surface of the ground. The pouring is 16 inches wide to accommodate the floor joists and stonework (Fig. 15-6).

There are no re-bars used other than that which are put 3 inches below the top surface of the poured concrete foundation. No

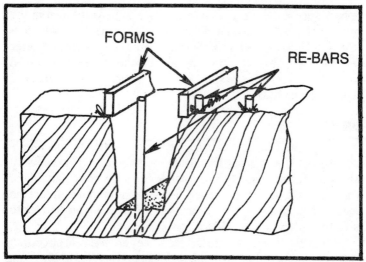

Fig. 15-5. Pour the concrete footing carefully.

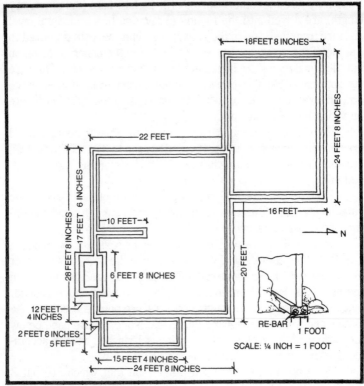

Fig. 15-6. A layout plan for the footing.

re-bars stick up above the concrete pour to be embedded in the stonework. This could be done, which would make for better construction. However, no cracks have appeared in the stonework after several years. This is because the stone in the stonework is placed correctly to avoid this cracking. Also, the footing is placed on a solid uniform gravel base.

SUBFLOOR

When the foundation forms are removed and the concrete is set, the subfloor is built. The plates are then put in place. Where wind is a problem, the plates are bolted to the concrete foundation. This was not done on these plates. The stonework would protect the house in Fig. 15-2 from blowing away. The plates are marked out to have the floor joists on 16-inch centers.

When the floor joists are installed, they are nailed in place with their crowns up, rather than with their cambra up (Fig. 15-7). When their ends are laid on the plate, they are sized. That is, their ends are

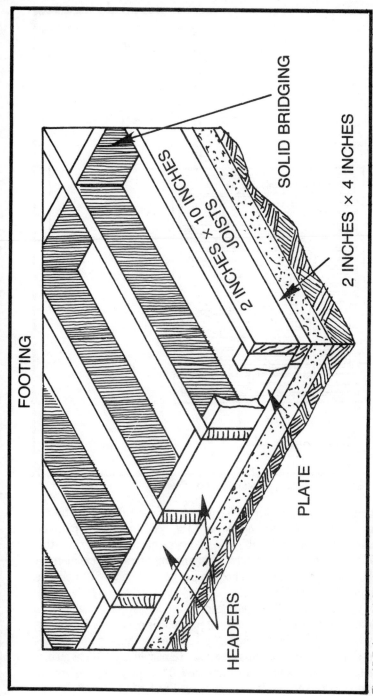

Fig. 15-7. Lay out joists in this manner.

205

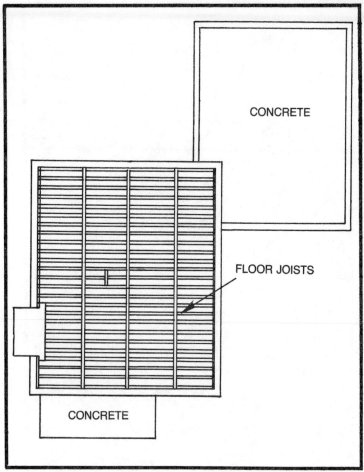

Fig. 15-8. This layout plan is for main floor joists.

planed to the same width. This insures that all the joists will be the same height when installed. Where the solid bridging is put, the joists will be even and level. A level floor is a must. The joists for this house were on 16-inch centers. There is a footing and foundation put in the center of the house to hold up the joists (Fig. 15-8). A plate is also placed on this foundation.

When the joists and the headers are in place, the subfloor is nailed. The ⅝-inch water-resistant plywood is used. It is not necessary to insulate or sound proof the subfloor as there is not a basement. The ground under this house has remained dry. The ⅝-inch, 4 by 8 foot plywood panels are staggered. This staggering makes the subfloor more secure. It will not spread wider in size.

206

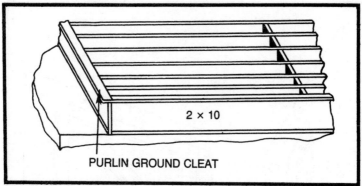

Fig. 15-9. Panels are installed against a purlin ground cleat.

When the subfloor is finished, the temporary stonework panel backing is built. Note the 2 × 4-inch cleat on the subfloor paneling. The panels are installed against this cleat at their bottom (Fig. 15-9). This keeps the stonework in straight alignment. It also leaves space between the stonework and the subfloor framing.

The panels are placed upright against 2 × 4-inch studs. A plate is nailed to the top of the studs. This plate will keep the stonework on the inside of the house in straight alignment. These studdings are held perpendicular by using 2 × 4-inch braces. The braces are placed against a 2 × 4-inch purlin nailed to the studding. The braces are placed 4 feet apart and nailed to cleats which are attached to the subfloor (Fig. 15-10).

After the panels are in place, the window and door bucks (frames) are nailed to the outside of the panels (Fig. 15-11). Care in measurements should be taken to have them put in the right places.

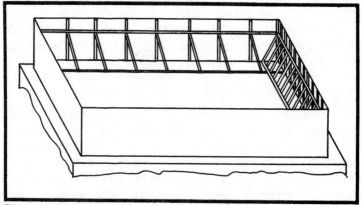

Fig. 15-10. Panels and braces are nailed in this manner.

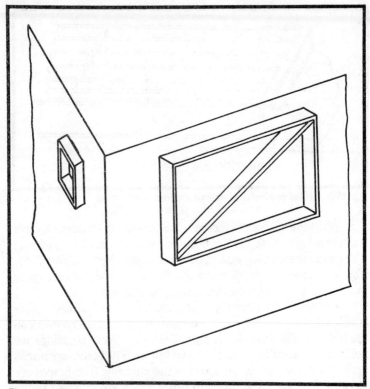

Fig. 15-11. Bucks are nailed to place on panels.

The stonework is set against them as the stone is set, the ties are nailed to the frames. This holds the buck and frames in place when the inside paneling is removed.

These bucks are braced on their insides to insure they will stay in proper horizontal and perpendicular positions.

After the window and door bucks and frames are put in place, only the outside work, such as patio, walkways, outdoor barbeque, and flower box are left to be done.

FLOOR AND ELEVATION PLANS

There is a floor plan for this house. This plan shows the walls of the house in correct dimensions. It locates where the doors and windows would go in the house. It designates the distance measurements from window centers and door openings from each other. The garage and the fireplace along with the walkways, patio, barbeque and flowerbox are shown. The different windows, doors, and openings are number-designated for reference as to size, kind and

208

quality. These can be listed. All dimension measurements are shown on the floor plan.

On the floor plan (generally called blue print floor layout detail by many construction men) in Fig. 15-12 are the measurements as to the size of the house, the measurements for windows and doors, the foundation width, the fireplace footing size and the designating numbers of detail references. The porch and the garage size are also shown along with the width of the stonework. Also refer to Fig. 15-13.

Windows generally are the same height at the tops. Some of the windows of this house are somewhat lower than the average door height. Some windows do not always have the same height sills.

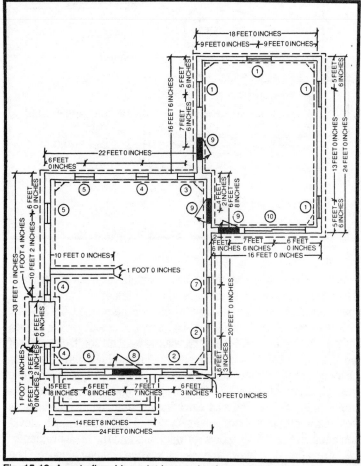

Fig. 15-12. A main floor blue print layout plan for a stone house.

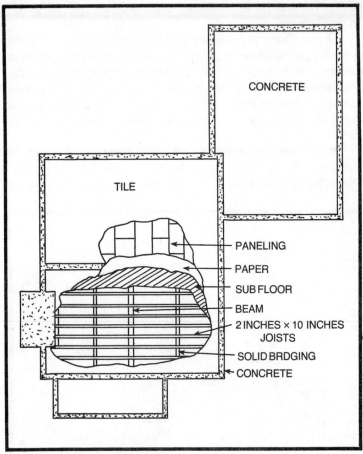

Fig. 15-13. Detail of the main floor.

Wall plans show the necessary designations, such as names of the various parts and materials used in the house construction. An open view is shown of the masonry part of the house (Fig. 15-14). This plan and all the elevation plans show the openings of windows and doors, porches, additions and walkways. The south elevation of the house, which does include the openings along with the measurements and window designations, is shown in Fig 15-15. The west elevation of the house (25.15) shows openings and measurements (Fig. 15-16). The east elevation presents all the openings as well as the porch, walkway and slab (Fig. 15-17). The north elevation detail in Fig. 15-18 shows the openings and the measurements.

Elevation drawings are necessary when building a house. The detail reference numbers refer to the window and door material list

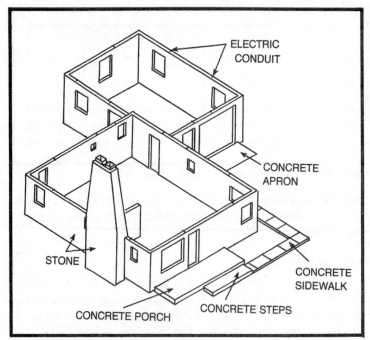

Fig. 15-14. Masonry plan for a stone house.

or to a detail of construction as is presented for the construction method of building.

There are also, roof elevation plans. These include besides measurements, the materials needed. They show where the measurements are used.

North Roof Elevation

The north elevation of the roof on this house shows location of materials. The fireplace stack is of stone with tile liners. This roof is

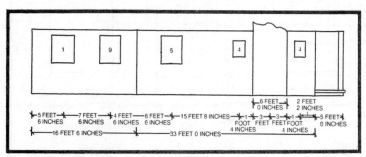

Fig. 15-15. South elevation for the house.

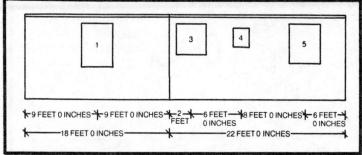

Fig. 15-16. West elevation for the house.

covered with asphalt shingles laid on 30-pound felt. The gable end is stuccoed on galvanized stucco metal lath laid on 30-pound felt paper (Fig. 15-19).

East Roof Elevation

The east roof elevation displays the various kinds of materials used on the house (Fig. 15-20). It also shows the gable end windows. The porch roof is of ashphalt shingles, as is the house, and it has a pitch roof on the front and sides. The house proper has a 5/12 pitch roof. The garage part is a combination 5/12 pitch roof. All the asphalt shingles are laid on 30-pound felt paper. The chimney stack is of stone. The chimney flashing is of 16-gauge galvanized metal. It is made U-shaped to fit the chimney stack. Windows are shown.

South Roof Elevation

The southern roof elevation plan depicts the various materials used (Fig. 15-21). The roof is of asphalt shingles. The fireplace stack is of stone. The back porch half gable end is stuccoed.

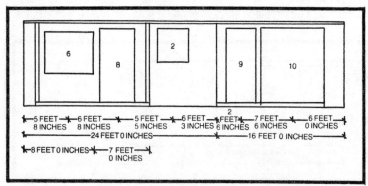

Fig. 15-17. The east elevation shows the porch, walkway and slab.

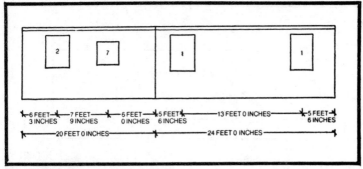

Fig. 15-18. A north elevation detail.

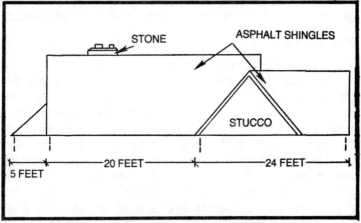

Fig. 15-19. This north roof elevation detail shows needed materials.

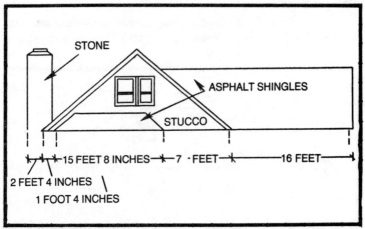

Fig. 15-20. The east roof elevation detail shows gable end windows.

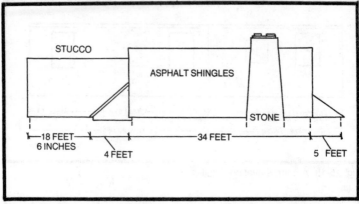

Fig. 15-21. The south roof elevation plan shows the stone fireplace stack.

West Roof Elevation

The west elevation showing the upper part of the house above the stone walls depicts the gable ends of the house proper and the garage (Fig. 15-22). The roof has asphalt shingles. Gable ends are stucco-coated on stucco galvanized metal lath. The mullion windows are placed flush with the sheathing. Their trim covers 30-pound felt placed on the sheathing. Measurements are shown in the elevations.

The gable end drawing of the upstairs shows the shape, size and construction (Fig. 15-23). The main floor plan includes the many parts of the floor construction (Fig. 15-24). The upstairs floor plan shows sizes of the rooms, clothes closets, hallway and stairs (Fig. 15-25).

Plate

The method of fastening the plate on which the ceiling joists (or upstairs floor joists) set is shown in Fig. 15-26. Note the anchor bolts

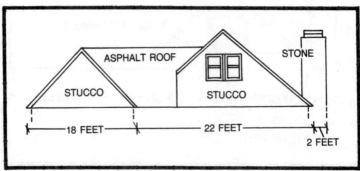

Fig. 15-22. A west roof elevation detail.

214

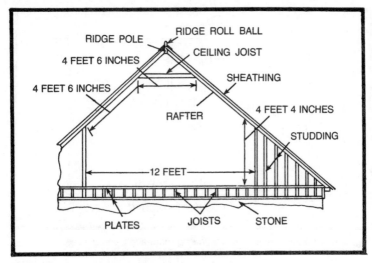

Fig. 15-23. Shown is the gable end of the upstairs.

holding the plate secure to the stonework. Then, too, the stone wall is solid where the anchor bolts are placed. The plate that carries the joists is 2 × 12 inches, the same width as the stone wall is thick.

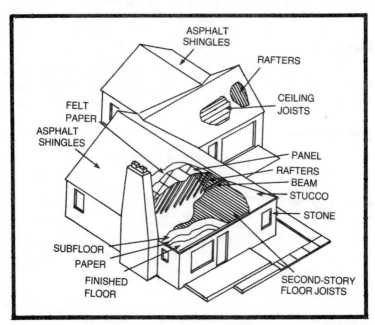

Fig. 15-24. This house plan gives a detailed look at more construction steps.

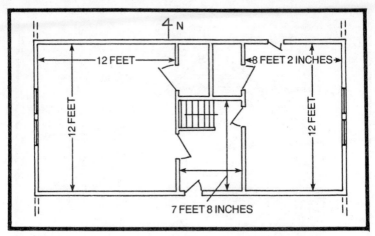

Fig. 15-25. An upstairs floor plan showing room and hallway sizes.

MATERIALS

For the house we are discussing, 6½ tons of stone were hauled to the building site. About 12½ yards of concrete were used for footings, foundation, floor and walkways. Three yards of graded sand were delivered. Thirty-six sacks of cement and four sacks of lime were ordered; 70 pounds of mortar color were used. The materials in Table 15-1 were purchased.

RAFTER DETAIL

The method used in this house to install the rafters on the plate is shown in Fig. 15-27. The number designations are given. The pitch of the roof is shown. The plate is in place and secured with

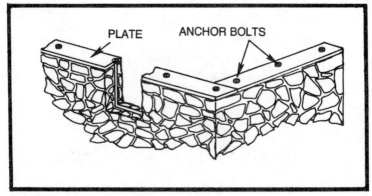

Fig. 15-26. Plates are fastened in this manner.

Table 15-1. Materials, other than stone, required for the house.

66—2 × 10 × 12	99—⅝ inches— 4 × 8 Plywood
27— 2 × 10 × 14	14—¾ inches— 4 × 8 Particle Board
2— 2 × 14 × 16	8 Rolls Felt
8— 2 × 6 × 12	20 squares of shingles
79— 2 × 6 × 16	4— #1 32 × 48 Windows
1—2 × 6 × 8	2— #2 32 × 42 Windows
40— 2 × 4 × 16	1— #3 32 × 32 Windows
21— 2 × 4 × 12	3— #4 16 × 24 Windows
35— 2 × 4 × 14	2— #5 32 × 40 Windows
66— 2 × 4 × 10	1— #6 60 × 48 Windows
54— 2 × 4 × 8	4— #7 32 × 36 Windows
4—5/4 × 12 × 12	1— #8 3–6 × 6-6 Door, 1 ¾ inches
1— 5/4 × 12 × 8	2— #9 2-8 × 6-6 Door, 1 ¾ inches
8— 1 × 8 × 12	4— #10 32 × 40 Windows
16— 1 × 8 × 16	2 Closet Doors 2— 4 × 8, 1 ⅜ inches
8— 1 × 4 × 12	7 Inside Doors 2-6 × 6-6, 1⅜ inches
16— 1 × 4 × 16	62— 4 × 8 Sheetrock, ⅝ inches
20— 1 × 4 × 10	

anchor bolts. Headers are in their proper places. The trim and various boards are properly placed.

The tail of rafters vary according to the requirement of different construction men, architects, engineers or owners. The overhang trim will also vary, but will always accommodate the various rafter tail lengths. These are shown in their proper proportion.

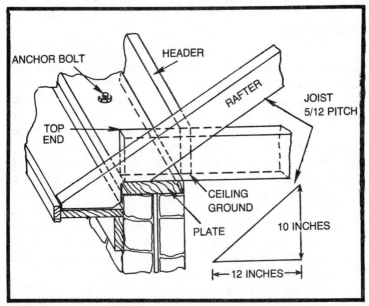

Fig. 15-27. Rafters are nailed to floor joists.

Fig. 15-28. Saw-cut stone is usually pitched with a stone set and hammer.

These rafters were notched. However, unnotched rafters are also used in some construction. They are nailed to the floor joists for securing. The notched rafters can be more securely nailed to the plate as well as the rafters and floor or ceiling joists. Some carpenters like a wide plate for a ground, but this may necessitate notching the bottom of the joists or hacking off the top end of the joists.

STONE CUTTING

After the stone for the house is on the building site, the stone shaping commences. The sizes of stone required depend upon the stone to a great extent. The kind of stonework also depends on the stone at hand and the required stonework. This stone is rough and quarried.

Stone used in this house varies in size and shape. Some of the stones are small, that is 3 inches through, and some are as thick as 2 feet through. This stone could be sawed with a handsaw when it was taken from the top of a mountain south of Livingston, Montana. It hardens in the air and continues to get harder as time goes on.

The bottom (or outside wainscot) of the stonework is sawed with a power saw using a diamond blade. Water is used on the saw blade to keep the diamond blade cool. The stone is sawed in certain sizes to be set in as near an ashlar bond as possible. An ashlar pattern is not followed in the setting of the stone.

The upper part of the stone house walls is random-set rubble. However, the stone is shaped with a hammer to fit at the time of setting. A bricklayer's hammer, or a scutch, and a stone hammer are used to shape the stone. With the use of a stone set the arris is wrought true. The face of the stone is wrought with a pick and hammer. In some cases, the scutch is used. The stone hammer (spalling hammer) helps make small stone out of the larger ones.

The stones used for the wainscot are cut in 9½, 7½, 3½ and 1½-inch widths with the diamond blade power saw. The lengths vary and are generally cut off when the stones are set. All the stones are arris pitched, either with the use of the stone set of just the bricklayer's or stonesetter's hammer.

Saw-Cut Stone

The saw-cut stone is arris pitched, generally, using a stone set and hammer (Fig. 15-28).

Hammer-Pitched Stone

When using the different tools to pitch stone, it is a must to choose the right tool as well as the right sized tool (Fig. 15-29). Should a too heavy tool be used when pitching stone, the cut will be very uneven. If a lightweight tool is used, the cut will be too small and the hammering will have to be watched very carefully. Practice will always help when a tool is chosen.

The hammer chosen when pitching stone has a lot to do with the tool used. A test trial on a particular stone to be wrought will dictate the tools to use, as no two stones are alike in toughness or hardness.

The degree a tool is held has something to do with the pitching (Fig. 15-30). Too much of a degree from straight will pitch out a small amount. Not enough degree will make a straight cut. Just the right amount of slant can be obtained through practice.

Fig. 15-29. Run tests with different hammers before selecting the one that is just right for pitching stone.

Fig. 15-30. It takes practice to hold tools at the right angle for pitching.

A pitching set has a slant bevel on its cutting edge. This slant should always be set on the stone with the longest and sharp edge next to the main body of the stone. The bevel will have a tendency to throw out the waste that is cut off.

A heavy stout table is used when wroughting the stone (Fig. 15-31). It has a soft ½-inch masonite top. This top takes the sharp jar when the stone is hit.

A sand box 2 feet square having 2 or 3 inches of sand in it does make a good cutting table on which to cut stone. Anything that will give as a stone is cut can be used. Stone can be wrought on the ground, but this puts the stonemason in an awkward position, especially if this cutting should last all day. The table should be at a height that will put the average size stone being wrought at least just below the waist line.

SILL STONE BRICK

Brick for the sills is made of stone. The stone is taken from the stone pile according to color and hardness. These stones can be a reddish pink to a near white color. Some of the stones selected for the house described in this Chapter were mottled with a variegated mixture of these colors. Uniform color is best and should be as dark as possible. The deeper reddish color is fine.

The stones are tested with a hammer for hardness. Take a claw hammer, or a lightweight stone hammer, and tap the stone. The sharper the ringing sound, the harder the stone. The pinging ring will vary from a dull to a sharp sound.

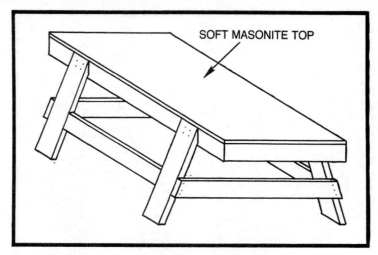

Fig. 15-31. A heavy table is used when wroughting stone.

It is best to hold the stone free and hit it a quick, light blow with the hammer (Fig. 15-32). The stone can be hit when setting on the celotex, rubber or soft masonite-topped stone table. Should the stone be struck with a hammer when it is in a pile of stones the ringing sound will not be as distinguishable for testing hardness.

When wroughting stone on a table like this, the soft masonite helps hold the stone. It gives to the hammer blows and the stone will be easier to shape. Stone generally cracks at the angle where the pressure is applied, unless there is a natural plane division in the stone.

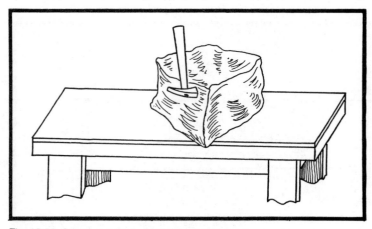

Fig. 15-32. Stones can be tested for hardness.

Fig. 15-33. The proper way to pile stone according to size and shape.

When the stone is ready for setting, it should be piled according to its size and shape (Fig. 15-33). It is more readily found when setting commences.

The unwrought stone is set on the table and hacked into slabs approximately 3 to 4-inches thick. This is done with a chisel and hammer (Fig. 15-34).

These slabs are cut on the diamond blade power saw into brick (Fig. 15-35). The bricks are cut to uniform sizes, near the sizes of standard clay brick. Sill brick sizes are shown in Fig. 15-36.

Fig. 15-34. Stone can be split with a chisel and hammer.

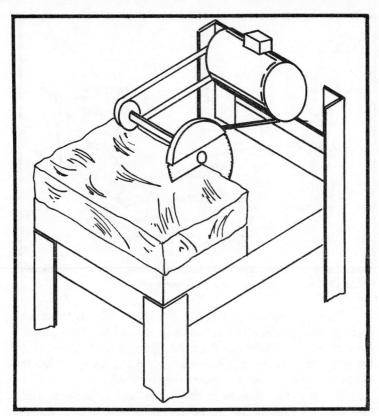

Fig. 15-35. A diamond blade power saw cuts slabs into brick.

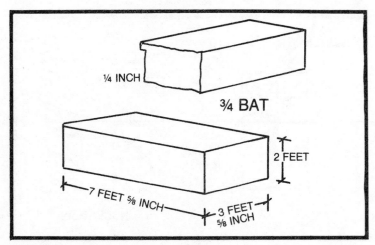

¼ INCH

¾ BAT

2 FEET

7 FEET ⅝ INCH

3 FEET ⅝ INCH

Fig. 15-36. Sill brick should be sized carefully.

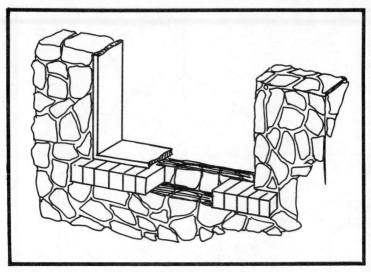

Fig. 15-37. The brick extends beyond the frame sills.

The bricks are set as close to the sills of the frames in the opening as is possible. They are set last, after all the house proper stonework is set. The stonework of the house under the openings is set below the opening sills approximately 5 inches, which leaves ample room for the setting of the stone brick sills.

Note that the sill stone brick extends beyond the frame sills (Fig. 15-37). These stone bricks are set to the inside insulation center. The inside stonework is set to the frame sills.

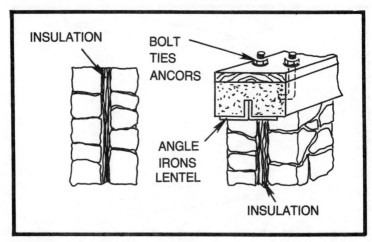

Fig. 15-38. Use insulation in wall construction.

When setting the sill stone brick, it is best to start setting from the center of the sill. Set the stone brick from there to the jambs. Measure and mark for each one so there will be full-width stone brick in the sill.

Figure 15-38 shows the construction of the lintels. The lintel shown here is two 4 by 3-inch angle irons bolted or welded together.

SETTING STONE

The corners of the house (lead) are set first (Fig. 15-39). Two lines are generally used, one on the inside and one on the outside (Fig. 15-40). This method of keeping the stonework plumb and level

Fig. 15-39. Corners are set first.

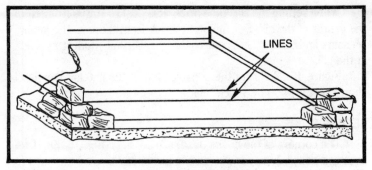

Fig. 15-40. Lines help keep the stonework level.

is generally used on jobs. This method is not employed on the stonework on this house, but a line is used on the outside of the stonework as it is laid. On the outside, paneling is used.

The stone walls of this house have insulation in the hollow wall part. Insulations put in place when setting the stone. The inside stone is set against the perpendicular panel (Fig. 15-41). The stone is held at 3½ to 4-inches in depth to the panel. When this inside stove is approximately 16 inches high, the insulation is placed against it. The outside stone is then set against the insulation and kept at an average of 4 inches deep. Ties are then placed across the insulation to hold the stone walls together.

The outside line comes in handy to keep the stone plumb. The line is at least 16 inches above the stone setting. By looking down from this line to the set stone, the stone being set can be kept in alignment.

Some foam insulations are hard and some are soft. Wool insulation, such as spun glass, could be used. The insulation for the stonework of this house is 1-inch thick and in panel form. It is cut into narrow 16″ widths or less. This size is easier to handle. Anchor ties are spaced 16 inches apart, vertically as well as longitudinally, to hold the inside stonework and the outside together. The stonework is solid next to the openings and next to the plate.

MORTAR

The mortar used when setting stone on this house is proportioned carefully. The lime (hydrated) is soaked in water to a thick putty. It is ready for use in two days. A sack of lime is puttied at a time. It is kept covered. Portland cement is put on the layer of graded sand. The color (black and red mixed to a brown) is scattered on the cement. Sand, cement and color is well chopped from one end

226

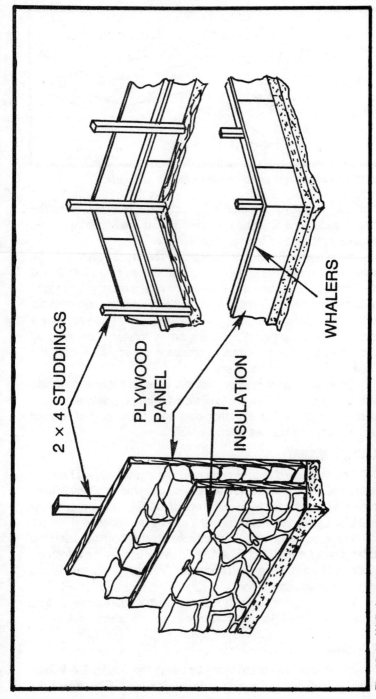

2 × 4 STUDDINGS

PLYWOOD PANEL

INSULATION

WHALERS

Fig. 15-41. Walls have insulation in the hollow wall section.

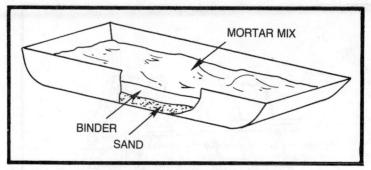

Fig. 15-42. Use the right proportions of mortar mix and water.

of the mortar box to the other before the water is added. When the water is added, the lime putty is mixed in. Just enough water is used to make a rather stiff mortar (Fig. 15-42).

When using the mortar for setting the stone, care must be taken not to splash the stonework below. Sloppy (thin) mortar will run down on the stonework. The color in the mortar will, in many cases, separate and follow the water as it seeps out when stone is set on the mortar, if thin mortar is used. Therefore, it is best to use heavy or thick mortar. When using heavy mortar, care must be taken to firmly seat the stone to eliminate any voids between the mortar and the stone being set.

Heavy stone used in stonework will, when set one on the other, force the mortar out from the lower mortar joints. It is best to set a course of stone at a time, rather than one course atop of courses having unset or semi-set mortar joints.

ELECTRIC WIRING

An electrician should be employed to wire the house. There are certain building codes to follow when wiring a home. It is best to have an electrician do this wiring. Electricians will follow the regulations called for by the electric companies and zoning codes.

The stonework should accommodate the conduit, inlet and outlet boxes for the electric wiring. In many houses the telephone wiring, and sometimes the radio and TV wiring, will have to be considered and allowed for.

Wiring plans are generally followed when wiring a house. These are not considered here and will not be shown in this book.

PLUMBING

A plumber can be called on to plumb the house. He follows plumbing methods and zoning code requirements. This keeps the plumbing within the regulations of the health department. When setting the stonework, allowance has to be made for such plumbing pipes as were in or through the stonework.

The plumbing layout will not be discussed in this book. Each house has its own plumbing layout to conform to the building regulations as well as to the owner's and builder's desires.

HEATING AND WATER

The heating furnace is installed under the stairs by a furnace man. A "lowboy" furnace can be used. The furnace man for the house in Fig. 15-2 had his workmen run hot air and cold air ducts to and from the furnace. Every room in the house was taken care of adequately. This furnace could be regulated. The heat could be controlled at the grate for each room or at the furnace. It is a good natural gas furnace hot air heating system.

The water for this house comes from a deep well. The water tastes good and has a pure test. A submerged pump is used. The water from this well comes through an underground 1¼-inch galvanized pipe. The house also has access to city water.

The well pump can be run either with 110 volt or 220 volt electric current. The master valve can turn off the well water to the city water. Generally, the well water is used for irrigating the yard, trees and garden. City water is used for the house.

FIREPLACE

The fireplace in this house has a metal heatform unit in it. This unit is a circulating unit having inlets for cold air and outlets for hot

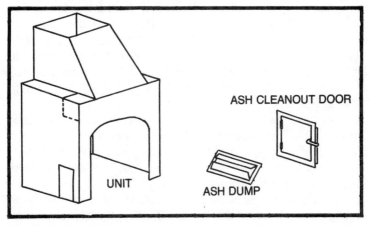

Fig. 15-43. A typical fireplace unit.

ASH CLEANOUT DOOR

ASH DUMP

UNIT

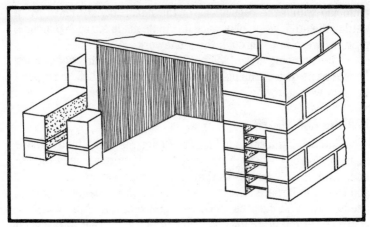

Fig. 15-44. Set stone carefully.

air. The grates (louvers) are of stone. There are no fans in the unit to circulate the air. Temperature does the circulating. Either wood or coal can be burned for heat in this fireplace. The house has actually been heated for one month in winter by using only the fireplace.

Fireplace Unit

The size of the fireplace unit has a 34-inch opening in width. It is installed with an opening height of 26 inches and a depth of 22 inches for the firebox (Fig. 15-43). Brick is laid around the fireplace unit up to the liner. Stone is set around the brick-covered fireplace unit (Figs. 15-44 and 15-45).

The front of the fireplace to the mantel and from the hearth to the ceiling is set with stone and secured by the ties left in the stonework and brickwork (Fig. 15-46). This face stonework can be removed and replaced with some other masonry facework if desired. The outside and sides of the fireplace are built together along with the house stonework. The fireplace unit is set in when the stack part of the fireplace was started. Liner is installed and built around with stone at that time. Figure 15-47 depicts the stack.

The upper part above the stone house wall is tapered to lose a foot in width. The side next to the house and away from the house is not battered in from perpendicular. This sloping gives better appearance to a stack, especially a stack on a house. It does not have the appearance of tipping out to either side.

The chimney liner starts at the smoke chamber and continues beyond the top of the stack (Fig. 15-48). A 2 or 3-inch projection of the liner looks best. However, many stonemasons give the liners as

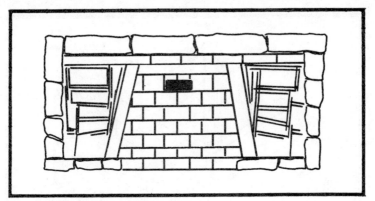

Fig. 15-45. Stone is set around the brick.

much as 12 to 28 inches height above the stack. There is not much downdraft where the house in Fig. 15-2 was built, so it was not unnecessary to build a cap on the chimney stack. A cap is useful also

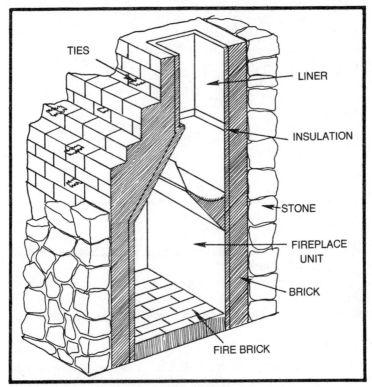

Fig. 15-46. Stone and brick layout for the fireplace.

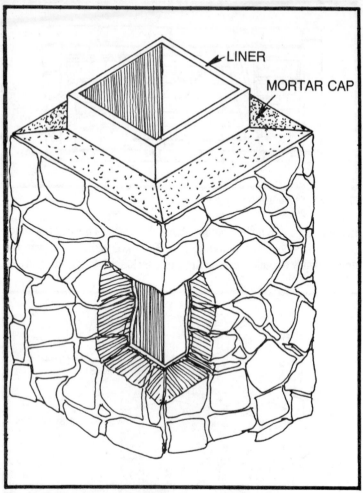

Fig. 15-47. The stone is set to the liner.

where there is a great quantity of snowfall. The cap keeps snow from getting into the stack liner.

The mantel of the fireplace can be installed with lumber or planking. The hearth is made of fabricated stone (Fig. 15-49). It is made by the methods covered in this book for making artificial stone.

Louvers

The louvers (air grates) for the inlets and outlets are made of stone. They are cut with a diamond blade saw. In size they are cut ½ by 1½ by 6-inches long and set in mortar at their ends (Fig. 15-5).

232

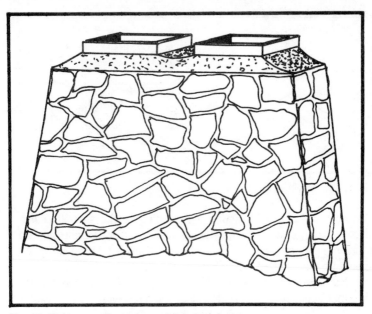

Fig. 15-48. Liner continues beyond the stack top.

The chambers back of the louvers (grates) are plastered smooth with the same mortar used to set the stone. Louvers are best installed during the stone setting of the finished face of the fireplace breast. The mortar for plastering should be thinned down some. This will make the plastering much easier. Mortar should be troweled smooth (Fig. 15-51). Two coats are generally used. The

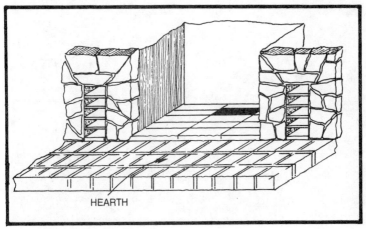

HEARTH

Fig. 15-49. This hearth is made with fabricated stone.

233

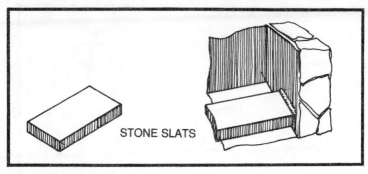

Fig. 15-50. Install louvers in this manner.

first coat will alleviate suction which will give the second coat a chance to set, before the moisture is sucked out by the masonry on which the plaster is applied. Masonry on which plastering is applied should be well wetted down before plastering.

Both the cold air intake at the bottom of the fireplace and the hot air outlet vent above are treated alike when installing louver grates.

Fig. 15-51. A trowel is used to smooth mortar.

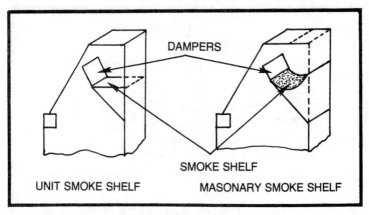

Fig. 15-52. The smoke shelf is rounded.

The bottom cold air intake openings sometimes have fans placed to or installed in them. They force in air. The hearth in the firebox is laid with firebrick as is the smoke chamber. The smoke shelf is rounded, not flat (Fig. 15-52). This method helps to direct the incoming air from the top of the chimney stack and starts it up the chimney liners to take out the smoke.

Angle Iron

A 4 × 4 × 42-inch angle iron is used over the firebox opening. It creates a 26-inch high opening.

Another angle iron is used on which to set the liner on the side next to the house (Fig. 15-53). This angle iron is 4 feet long and otherwise the same size of the 42-inch one.

These angle irons are padded at their ends with spun insulation. The purpose is to leave space for the angle irons expansion due to heat.

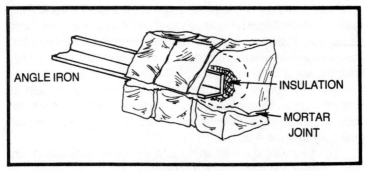

Fig. 15-53. Angle irons should be padded at the ends with insulation.

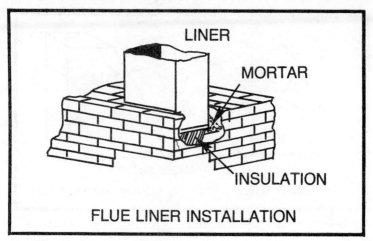

LINER

MORTAR

INSULATION

FLUE LINER INSTALLATION

Fig. 15-54. The liner is part of the masonry.

Angle irons should have a bearing of at least 4 inches at their ends. Where it is possible, a 6-inch extension at the ends is best. The masonry the irons set on will then stand the pressure of the load above.

Fireplace Layout

The fireplace layout has to be of a size, when a fireplace heatform unit is used, to accommodate the unit. An allowance should be made for the hot and cold air grates (louvers). Any extension of the fireplace face width can be made as required.

The fireplace should have a foundation large enough to accommodate not only the unit proper, but also the stone and brick required in its building. An outside fireplace back should have allowance in depth for a double thickness of stone or brick. This will help to eliminate condensation.

Note the space between the unit and the masonry work. This space of at least 1-inch is necessary to allow for expansion of the unit during use. If this is not done, the unit expansion could and has cracked masonry work. This space is also necessary when a firebrick firebox is built, as firebrick will expand when heated.

When firebrick is used in the hearth, the firebrick was dipped in a thin mortar and immediately set. Fireclay is best when it can be obtained. It is mixed with water to a cream thickness. No binder or sand goes into the mix.

The liner should not sit on the unit anywhere. It should sit on and be part of the masonry (Fig. 15-54).

Fireplace Breast Pattern

The pattern of placing stone in a fireplace front gives beauty to any fireplace. The stone in this fireplace was cut and laid out on the subfloor previous to setting. Note the stone pattern. The stone on the right is like the stone on the left which gives the stonework unique distinction (Fig. 15-55). Figure 15-56 shows a finished fireplace.

PATIO

The patio back of the house is of stonework construction (Fig. 15-57). This stone varies from 2½ to 4 inches in thickness and is of various sizes. It is random-laid like rubble. Excavation is only 16 inches deep. Course gravel is tamped in to bring the excavation up to

Fig. 15-55. A fireplace breast pattern.

Fig. 15-56. This fireplace is ready for a fire.

the surface level of the ground. The stone is set in a concrete pour having a 6-inch welded wire mesh reinforcing.

OUTDOOR BARBEQUE

The outdoor barbeque is placed on the out corner of the patio. See Fig. 15-58.

Barbeque Footing

Since a stone barbeque is heavy, a good footing is necessary (Fig. 15-59). The footing of this barbeque is of concrete. The foundation is stone. Fireboxes are lined with firebrick. The barbeque

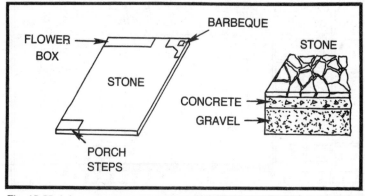

Fig. 15-57. Information for construction of a patio.

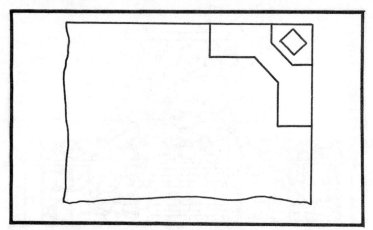

Fig. 15-58. The barbeque in this drawing is placed on the outside corner of the patio.

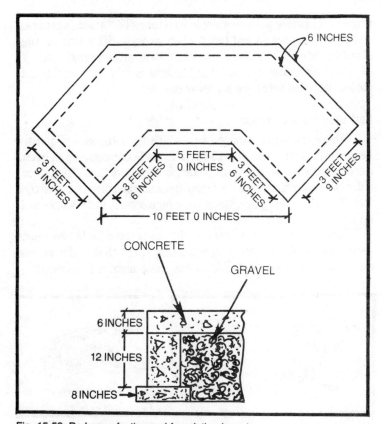

Fig. 15-59. Barbeque footing and foundation layout.

Fig. 15-61. Barbeque front elevation.

proper is of rubble stonework of ledge stone. This stone is hammer and stone set pitched and faced when wrought. The arris is truly shaped to where the stone can be set with its arris approximately ¾ of an inch from the mortar joints. Mortar is raked out evenly and tooled flat. The barbeque layout is detailed in Fig. 15-60.

Barbeque Front Elevation

There are various shaped fronts built for barbeques. One barbeque front is shown in Fig. 15-61. This barbeque contains an oven, a cooking place, some bottom grates, firebox doors, an ashpit door, a damper, ash pit, a place for wood and a storage place for charcoal fuel. It also has a fireplace. Its shape is for a corner, and it works well on the patio corner.

It is almost essential that the different units a barbeque needs should be procured before construction (Fig. 15-62). There are many sizes of units. Ample space for these units is necessary.

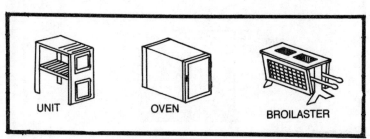

Fig. 15-62. Buy barbeque units before beginning construction.

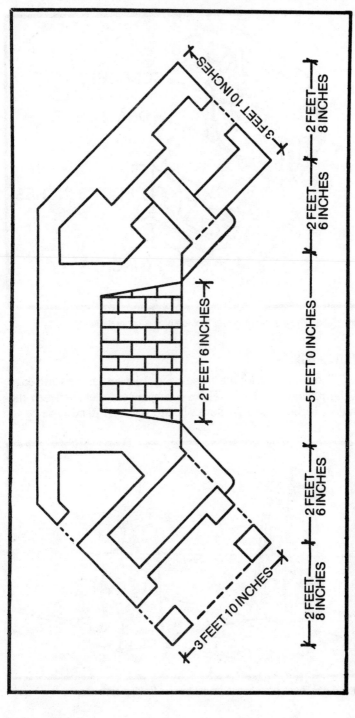

Fig. 15-60. The barbeque layout. Measure carefully.

241

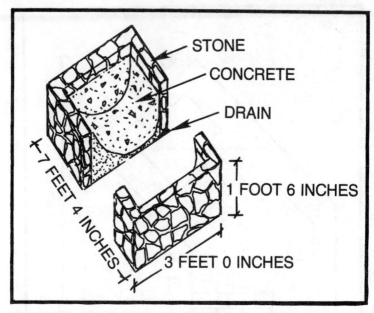

Fig. 15-63. The planter or flower box features a concrete lining.

FLOWER BOX

The flower box for the house in Fig. 15-2 sets at the south edge of the patio (Fig. 15-63). There is ample space left between the outdoor barbecue and the flower box to walk and stand while cook-

Fig. 15-64. These posts make an impressive looking entrance.

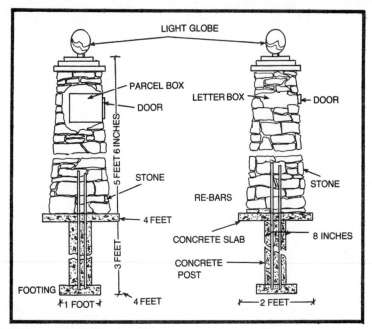

Fig. 15-65. Make sure the gate posts have a solid footing.

ing. The flower box is lined with concrete that is coved (rounded) at the bottom. Should the dirt be water-soaked and freeze in the winter, the dirt will heave up rather than expand out sideways and crack the stonework.

The drain in the flower box is at the middle and drains out on the ground rather than on the patio. The end next to the house is flashed to keep rain and snow from getting between the house and the flower box.

ENTRANCE GATE POSTS

The entrance to the walkway of this house has welcoming gate posts (Fig. 15-64). These gate posts have a good footing. Settling, if it occurs, will be even. Uneven settling will cause a post to get out of true perpendicular (Fig. 15-65).

One of these gate posts has a mail box. The other post has a package box installed in it. Both have electric lights on their taps.

Chapter 16
Contracting

I have been a contractor for over 30 years. I joined the bricklayers' and stonemasons' union and have been a member for over 30 years, also. I should know the construction business.

Anyone can contract. But if he understands and can estimate the requirements and materials of a job, he will be a successful contractor. If he does not, he will surely go by the wayside as many do.

To be a stonework contractor, you should have a knowledge of mathematics. You should understand the decimal system. The metric system is now ours, also. A contractor will not stay in the business of contracting stonework very long unless he can figure. The most important thing in contracting is the ability to estimate correctly, for estimating a job is nearly all figuring.

You should be familiar with the terms used in construction. You must know the names and uses of the materials of stonework. It is to your advantage to know what tools, hand and powered, are used in stonework construction.

You have to have good credit or capital on which to operate. Therefore, your best asset as a contractor is honesty and the ability to make every promise true. Dependability and promptness are necessary for every contractor to consider. These are things, along with your integrity and good judgement, that will see you through in your contracting business.

Many stonework contractors starting out lack business experience and the ability to estimate the costs of a stonework job. Many of them have been stonemasons, foreman, superintendents, or have worked in building construction. Some stonework contractors without business training go broke. They should have had business experience or capital to tide them over until they gained through contracting experience the knowledge a contractor should have.

Generally, a contractor without business experience will take jobs at such a low price that they would surely go broke unless they do much of the work themselves, and without wages or profit. They barely make a livelihood and would be far better off working for wages.

It is the low bidders, in most cases, that are forced to do inferior work to stay in business. These are the ones who ruin not only the contracting business of competent builders, but will ruin themselves and not do the stonework masons any good. When contractors do inferior work to stay in business long enough to learn the business of estimating, they are most likely to go out of the stonework business for lack of jobs.

BUSINESS ACUMEN

Stonework contracting is a business and business in any field should be carried on in an efficient manner. You should keep records of all stonework jobs. Quantity and costs of materials should be on record. Cash discounts should be noted and taken advantage of for future jobs. Estimates of all jobs should be kept. The names and addresses of workers should be listed for future hiring. All transactions and blue prints, along with the specifications of completed jobs, is well to keep for reference as to certain details one may need on a future job. Above all, and from the standpoint of staying in business, receipts of all expenditures should be kept.

Should you contract, there are so many things to consider before you actually enter the business of stonework contracting. You have to keep books and records, if you are going to be a small contractor. Should you endeavor to be a big contractor, you should have an office and all that goes with it. You will need office help, especially if you cannot tend to the office yourself. Depending on the size of your contracting business, your overhead expense will be large or small. This overhead expense will become a stable, fixed expense and may, percentagewise, enter into all job estimates, or it will have to come out of your yearly profit.

EXPENSES

Office rent and upkeep, heat, lights, office equipment, fixtures, telephone, office help, fire insurance, liability insurance, social security, taxes, unemployment compensation, etc., including depreciation, are necessary expenses.

Magazines, books, club dues, association dues, advertising interest, traveling expenses, fares, automobile and truck expenses, and possible legal expenses, are generally forced on contractors in one way or another.

Yearly expenses include contractor's salary, estimator's license and salary (unless the contractor does his own estimating), storage rents, general tool and equipment upkeep and repair (which cannot be charged off to a job), interest on contracting investment, etc. There is also the help cost necessary to carry on the contracting business, which cannot be charged off on any particular job.

Decisions will have to be made as to whether to hire union or non-union employees. If a union employer, you should understand the union regulations with which you will be required to comply. You should know and understand your subcontractors. Should you sublet parts of your job? Will you have to carry a subcontractor's bond as well as yours or will he be bonded?

Above all, correct estimates are a must when you are contrasting stonework. If you cannot estimate, it will be to your advantage to have office employees that can carry on this particular end of contracting. You should learn to check their work or you could go broke.

ESTIMATING

To estimate properly, you should understand the specifications, know how to read and check the measurements on the blue prints or plans, and be able to list kinds and quantities of material needed. You should know where to procure this material and what it costs, plus cost of placing it on the job. You should know where the material will go in the job, the time it will take to put it in the job and the cost of putting it there. A properly prepared estimate, the purchasing of materials, the careful way you sublet (if you sublet) and the way you manage the work on the job are all important and necessary things to take care of if your aim is to stay in business and make a profit. You will then have figured everything pertaining to the job in detail. Your bid will be correct and you will know exactly how you will stand on any job you may get, barring, of course, weather and strikes.

A material costs should be divided and placed with the particular kinds and quantities listed for certain parts of the job where they will be used. The labor costs should be listed along with the material costs. The reason for keeping these estimates, time, costs, etc., is that you will have a reference to consider when bidding on future jobs. And you will know just how well your estimates hold up after a job is completed. You can take that into consideration when bidding on jobs. The cost knowledge of the time it takes to perform a certain part of a job, taking into consideration the materials and conditions, is generally learned by cost records of previous stonework jobs performed.

Job conditions, temperature, the lay of the site, weather, room to place materials and working room and access to the job, should be taken into consideration when estimating. Always make an allowance for inconveniences which may, in time and money, run up the cost of a job.

Job costs should contain only a percentage of overhead expenses based on the total yearly overhead expense you may have during the year. Cost of the following should be in your estimate when figuring a job: building permit; survey of site cost; temporary roads; repair of any destruction which may happen during construction; cutting and repairing for other workers on the job; protection of work (finished and unfinished); removing and building sheds, shelters, etc.; removing and replacing masonry work; cleaning and removing rubbish, bucks and platforms; all temporary work such as decks; all carpenter expenses; trucking; drainage; bonding; social security and unemployment taxes; sales taxes; fees; fuel; electricity; breakage; time keeper; tool man; watchmen; water man; legal expense pertaining to the job; insurance; labor; superintendent; foreman, layout man, etc. Now don't forget contingencies, for there are always some.

One thing, you should consider very carefully is profit. That is the main reason for any contactor to be in the business. The total cost plus profit should include contingencies. If the amount for contingencies is too large, you may not get the job. And if your estimate is too low and your bid is low, then if you get the job, you will certainly be short on your contingencies. Then, too, high bidders will not get a job unless they have built up a reputation of honesty, dependability, service and good work.

Glossary

abutment: Part of a structure that directly receives thrust or pressure of an arch, vault, beam or strut.

adhesive strength: The strength mortar has for holding two stones together.

agglomerated mass: Matrix or binder and the aggregate mix, such as plaster, mortar and concrete.

aggregate: A hard, inert material in various size fragments, mixed with cementing material to form concrete, mortar or plaster. Particles of an agglomerated mass other than the binder and additives.

alignment: Construction units laid true to the line.

amalgamation: Mixing of various materials together in a unified mix, such as lime, cement, sand, color and water.

anchor: Metal rod or strap tie that gives stability to one part of a structure by making it fast to another part.

anchor grooves: Grooves cut in construction units to hold anchors.

angle bar: See **anchor.**

angle iron: Iron or steel cleat or brace used to hold together two parts whose faces are at an angle. It is also used to hold lintel units.

anta: Pier produced by thickening a wall at its termination; a pilaster attached to a wall.

arcade: Series of arches supported by columns or piers.

arch: Curved structural member spanning an opening and resolving vertical load pressure into horizontal or diagonal thrust.

arch cuttress: See **flying buttress.**

area: The surface within any set of lines, usually given in square units of measure.

arris: Sharp edge or angle formed by the meeting of two surfaces.

artificial: That which is not natural; man-made or synthetic.

ashlar: Squared and dressed stone; also, masonry of such stone.

ashlar line: Exterior line of an exterior wall above any projecting base.

axed work: Incisioned successive rows ⅛ to ¼-inch apart across a stone.

axis: In masonry arch work, the center or point from which a circle, arc, or intrados (and extrados) is formed or drawn on a template form.

backing: That part of the wall behind its face.

backing up: Laying the backing.

backset: A construction unit or course set back from the face of masonry work.

balanced: An even distribution of the load; proportionate, symmetrical.

basement: Lowest fundamental part of a structure that is above a footing; wholly or partly below ground level.

batten boards: Single or double boards placed outside the corner of an intended structure from which true lines are run.

batter: Deviation from the vertical.

batter stick: Tapered or pitched stick used with a level to build a battered wall. A tapered board attached to a spirit level.

beam: Main horizontal load-bearing member, supported by walls, columns, etc.

bearing stone: Stone supporting a load other than the units of which it is a part in the masonry work.

bearing wall: A wall or partition which supports weight.

bed: The top surface on which mortar is spread.

bed joint: Horizontal joint between construction units.

bed surface: Unfinished surface that carries the finish.

belt course: Horizontal course or band around pillars or engaged columns and stonework.

bench mark: Elevation mark or point of reference on a fixed object.

binders: Material such as cement, lime, etc., that produces cohesion of loose material, such as aggregate.

blind bond: Stone bond in which stone headers extend only halfway through the wall from face and backing; bonding in a wall that does not show on either side.

boasted work: Stone dress made with a boaster (wide cutting-edge chisel). Boasted marks are not kept in continuous rows across the stone.

bond: Systematic lapping of construction units in the face of mason for strength and appearance.

bonding course: Course in which construction units are laid transversely part way or entirely through a wall from the face.

boning rods: Rods to sight across to keep construction units level when laying them on a horizontal surface.

breadth: Breadth pertains to the face height of a stone in stonework.

breaking joint: Method of laying so that so that no two vertical joints will be immediately over one another.

breast wall: Wall built to sustain the face of a natural bank of earth.

bridge wall: Wall separating firebox from combustion chamber in a boiler setting.

broken range: Random laying; no true bond kept or desired.

buck: Rough, well-braced frame placed in a wall during construction.

buckstay: Either of two connected girders, one on each side of a masonry structure, to take the thrust of an arch.

bulging: Spreading or widening of a wall or pour generally caused by load pressure.

bush hammer: Hammer which is used for dressing stone and concrete.

buttress: Projecting masonry structure that resists lateral pressure at a particular point in one direction.

calcining: Heating stone for manufacturing cement or lime.

camber: Slight arch or curvature.

carving: Dressing a stone for stonework to a carved finish.

casting: A molded or cast construction unit.

caulking: Filling shrinkage cracks around window frames and expansion joints to make them weathertight.

cavity wall: Masonry wall built in two thicknesses separated by an air space; double-wall construction.

cell: Air space in a construction unit; a cellular cavity.

cement: A powder of alumina, silica, lime, iron oxide and magnesia burned together in a kiln and finely pulverized. When mixed with water, it forms a plastic mass that hardens by chemical combination. A binder of an agglomerated mass.

center: Temporary prop or support, similar to an underpin.

centering: Framework used temporarily, on which a mason may apply a compass, template or trammel rod when laying out arches. Timber falsework is part of the masonry arch during construction.

chase: Groove or channel left in masonry work for a pipe or conduit.

chimney: Hollow masonry stack that carries off smoke.

chimney breast: Projection of a chimney or fireplace from a wall into a room or projecting on the exterior of stonework.

chimney cap: Uppermost course or unit of a chimney stack. It is used to improve the draft by presenting an exit aperture to leeward.

chimney lining: Flue liner.

clastic: A conglomerate stone could be classified as a clastic stone. It is made up of other particles of stone, as is granite.

cleavage plane: Natural division of stone, in that two parts of the same stone will separate along the cleavage plane. It is in reality a seam in stone.

closer: The last construction unit laid in a course to close the course and maintain the bond.

cobblestone: Naturally-rounded stone, larger than pebbles and smaller than boulders; also, a cobble stonework.

cohesive strength: The cohesive strength of stonework pertains to one stone sticking to another and staying in place with the help of good mortar.

column: An ornamental or supporting pillar.

compass: An instrument or tool used to lay out work.

concrete: Hard, strong building material made of cement, aggregate and water.

conglomerate: Clastic sedimentary rock composed of rounded fragments cemented together by calcareous, siliceous or other material; an accumulation.

consistency: Degree of density or viscosity.

construction units: Brick, tile, block, stone, etc., used with or without mortar.

coping: Top-most course of a wall of masonrywork. It usually slopes to carry off water.

corbel: One or more courses of units stepped upward and outward from a vertical surface, supporting a super-incumbent weight.

corbie steps: On a gable, a series of steps rising to the ridgepole.

corner: Place of directional change of the walls or surfaces of a structure, such as inside or outside corners.

cornice: Top course of a wall, projecting horizontally, generally topped by a blocking course to weight it down and hold it in place.

course: One horizontal layer of laid construction units.

course bed: Top of the last course laid, upon which another course is to be placed.

cove: Concavity or recessed place in a structure.

cramps: Metal bars or irons bent at the ends to enter holes in construction units to hold them in place.

cross joint: Head joint between construction units in a course (true or variable) that connects the horizontal bed joints.

crowding the line: Called hard laying; building an overhanging wall.

crown: Extrados or vertex of an arch.

cubic measure: Unit or series of units for measuring volume.

cull: An inferior construction unit.

curing: Perfecting by chemical change and maintaining proper conditions of moisture and temperature. Having acquired its initial set and hardened, mortar is said to be in its curing stage.

curtain wall: Non-bearing wall that will not support girders or beams.

cut joint: Protruding mortar of cross and bed joints. It is cut off with a trowel.

depth: The distance from the face of the stone to the back of the stone in stonework.

diagonal thrust: The weight load of a stone construction wall may cause diagonal thrust, which is weight load pressure, as well as other pressure through a wall. Pressure causes stonework in the wall to bulge out either in the back or in the face of the stonework.

dimension stone: Sized stone of any size.

dipping: Dipping construction units into grout rather than spreading mortar on them before laying.

dowels: Anything used to hold construction units securely in placed when incorporated into masonry work.

draft: Difference in pressure between outside and inside air that draws air through a chimney.

drafts: Grooves cut to a plane on stone by a chisel and hammer. Drafts pertain to such work as weathering, margin drafts, winding, etc.

dressing: Working the face of a stone to the required finish; also, squaring a stone for ashlar.

dry stone: Stone laid without mortar (e.g., a dry-stone wall).

efflorescence: Powder or crust formed on the masonry surface by the flow of water. An incrustation due to contact with air. Dampness brings salts to surface.

elliptical arch: An arch shaped elliptically.

extrados: Upper, outer surace of an arch.

fabricated: A fabricated product is not a natural product. It is a manufactured product, such as a man-made stone or manufactured stone.

face: Outside surface of any construction unit or stonework that shows.

fat mortar: Mortar rich in a bonding material, such as cement, lime, etc., having less aggregate.

filling -in: Laying the center of a wall.

fireclay: Clay that is refractory and is able to withstand high temperatures without deforming. Better grades contain at least 35 percent alumina when fired. It is used as a mortar where refractory material is required.

firebrick: Brick which will withstand more heat then regular brick.

flat arch: Arch with straight or almost straight horizontal intrados and extrados.

flue: Inside passageway of a chimney stack for carrying off smoke.

flue liner: Flue tile.

flush: Bring a construction unit even (flush) with the surface of masonry work.

flushing: Slushing mortar into joints with a trowel.

flying buttress: Straight inclined masonry arch spanning an opening passageway to a solid pier. It is used to take up the thrust in stonework.

footing: Substructure or bottom unit of a wall or column.

form: Shaped temporary holder that retains an agglomerated mass until it is set hard enough to sustain its own weight and hold its shape.

foundation: Supporting part of a wall or structure, usually below ground level and including footings.

frame high: Masonry work laid to the level of a framed opening; specifically, the top of a frame.

gable ends: The gable end is the end of a building that extends from the eaves to the apex of the roof.

gallery: Roofed space open at the sides; also called an arcade or cloister.

galleting: Pressing stone pebbles into the face mortar joint for strength or appearance.

gauged putty: Putty stuff, each batch of which is mixed thin and in the same proportions to secure even setting.

gauged work: Forming, shaping, or proportioning of material, as voussoirs in arches.

gingerbread work: Ornate masonry with mixed kinds of construction units.

gothic arch: Pointed arch with a joint or key stone at its apex.

graded aggregate: Graded aggregate contains various particles of sand and gravel the mixture of which leaves particles of sand and gravel, the mixture of which leaves very little voids between the particles. Therefore, when a binder is mixed with the aggregate with water to start the chemical action, this mix will have very little voids.

graded sand: Graded sand contains various particles of sand, the mixture of which leaves very little voids between the particles. Mortar made when using this sand as an aggregate will make the best mortar.

grout: Mortar thin enough to pour. Coarse plaster coating a wall and later studded with small stones; used when setting some wrought stone.

haunch: That portion of an arch between skewback or springing and crown of an arch.

hawk: Small board or metal sheet with a handle on the underside; used to hold mortar.

head joint: Vertical joint between units in a course.

headway: Clearance below an arch.

hearth: Floor of a fireplace. Extends into the firebox as well as in front.

herringbone bond: Masonry bond in which construction units in adjacent rows slope slightly in reverse direction.

honed: A stone that is wrought smooth by sanding, grinding, or planing.

horseshoe arch: An arch shaped like a horseshoe.

horizontal thrust: Horizontal thrust is similar to diagonal thrust with the exception that horizontal thrust is lengthways of a stoneworked wall. To avert this thrust to a certain extent, reinforcing is put in a wall or, toggles and clamps are used.

hydrated lime: Slaked lime.

impervious: Not allowing entrance or passage through.

impost: The stone where the arch rests at the spring line.

in-corners: Corners at the inside angle of the outside walls of a structure.

initial set: The first taking up of water and achieving semi-hard condition.

insert: Setting or building of other units into the face of a wall or structure.

interlocking: Bonding construction units by lapping.

intrados: Interior curve of an arch; soffit.

inverted arch: Arch with the crown downward; used in foundations, sewers and tunnels.

jack arch: A flat arch. Also, a temporary, poorly constructed arch.

jamb: Side of an opening in a wall.

joggle: V-shaped sinking in the side of all the stone of the top course at the head or cross joints.

joint: Space between two adjacent units held together by mortar.

jointer: A tool used for joint finish work or jointing.

Keene's cement: Hard-finish gypsum plaster to which alum has been added.

keystone: Construction unit at the crown of an arch; the apex unit.

lacing course: Bonding the inside of unbonded stonework with a slabstone, as well as horizontal bands laid in bond rubble or cobble stonework.

lagging: Wooden strips for transferring to the center form the weight of an arch under construction.

lateral thrust: Sidewise movement caused by load pressure. This can cause stone in a wall to slip out of place if not protected when laid.

laying to bond: Keeping the bond plumb and true.

lead: Laying ahead or in advance of the line at the ends of the line for the purpose of having lead units as a guide and a place to attach the line.

lean mortar: Mortar that lacks enough binder.

lewis: Dovetailed tenon that fits into a dovetail mortice in a stone to lift the stone.

lime: Calcium carbonate; a binder.

line: String stretched taut from lead course to lead course. Used as a guide when laying construction units.

linear foot: One-foot distance along a straight line.

lintel: Horizontal architectural member spanning an opening and carrying the load above it.

low gothic arch: A squatty gothic arch.

lipped: Construction unit laid with its lower face edge protruding from the plumb face of the masonry work.

lock: Method of securing a laid unit.

mantel: Beam, stone, or arch supporting masonry above a fireplace. Fireplace finish covering front and sides of the chimney. Also, the ornamental shelf above a fireplace opening.

marginal line: The margin perpendicular outside line of the face of a structure.

measuring box: Box holding one cubic foot of material; used to mix proportions.

models: Casts used to copy, or to shape a plastic mix.

mortar: Plastic building material made of aggregate, binder and water.

mortar board: The board on which mortar is put for the stonemason.

muriatic acid: Commercial grade of hydrochloric acid; used as a masonry wash when diluted with water.

natural bed stone: Stone placed in a structure horizontally with its stratification.

neat cement: Pure cement and water (no aggregate).

niche: Recess in a wall.

nogging: Stonework filling open spaces of a wood frame, as between rafters, joists, etc.

obtuse corner: Corner with more than a 90 degree angle and less than a 180 degree angle between its walls.

offset: A construction unit or course of masonry set back from the face of the unit, or course, on which it is set.

ogee arch: Arch in which the intrados form two contrasting ogee or S curves that meet in a point at the apex.

oriel: Semi-hexagonal opening, projecting from a wall and supported by a corbel.

outrigger: Projecting beam that supports a scaffold.

out-corner: Corner outside of a structure, the flared joining walls of which are not more than 180 degrees apart.

overhand work: Setting stonework (in and outside faces) from one side of the wall.

overhang work: Wall face with corbeled cornice or outward battered wall.

overhead work: Work above the height of a mason.

panel: Sunken or raised section of a surface, set off by molding or other margin.

parapet: Low wall for protection or decoration generally placed along the edge of a roof or terrace.

pargetting: Plastering the inside of the chimney flue and smoke chamber to give a smooth surface and help the draft. Also, plastering the inside of a hollow wall.

party wall: Wall or partition between two adjoining properties, half its thickness on either property.

patching: Repairing.

peach basket: Temporary template form used when building the head of a large chimney stack.

pebble: Small, hard aggregate, or spall, placed in the mortar bed when setting stone. It holds the laid stone in place; between 5/32 and 2½ inches in diameter.

peening: Dressing of the face of a stone with a peen hammer.

perch: Measure of stone which is commonly 16½ by 1½ by 1 foot.

perpend: Large unit extending through a wall as a binder and appearing on both sides.

piano basket: An outside swinging scaffold.

pier: Vertical brickwork that supports the end of an arch, lintel or beams.

pilaster: A structural pier which projects a third or less of its width from the wall. It may or may not be load-bearing.

pitch: A slope from zero height at one end to inches or feet at the other end (e.g. pitch of a roof). Also, stone is pitched for the purpose of securing a true arris.

plastic: Capable of being molded or shaped; a pliable mass agglomerate.

plinth: Square block stone serving as a base of a column, wall or other structure.

plumb: Small weight (Bob) attached to a line which indicates vertical direction.

plumb bond: Masonry bond in which corresponding joints of a bond are in vertical alignment.

plumb rule: Narrow board with plumb line and bob. A measuring rule divided into various size elevations of course heights considered as standard.

pointing: Filling in missed places in joints, striking or tooling the joint, or removing excess mortar with a brush.

polishing: Smoothing, slicking and shining the finished surface of any masonry unit or material.

Portland cement: Hydraulic cement made of finely pulverized clinker produced by calcining to incipient fusion. A mixture of argillaceous and calcareous materials; a binder.

precast: An artificial unit. A mold, cast, etc., made before its use.

pressure: Pressure is exerted by weight load, whether as a wall load (dead or alive) or lateral force.

pudding stone: Congolmerate.

pugging: Filling with sound-absorbng morter.

quoin: Corner construction unit.

rabbeting: Making a groove, principally in stone.

racking bond: Diagonal bond.

raggles: Grooves or raked-out joints for flashing.

rake: Remove mortar from a joint before it sets. An inclined face or raked end of a wall.

rangework: Ashlar laid in horizontal courses.

recess: Niche.

relieving arch: Arch over a lintel or incorporated in the wall. It relieves or distributes weight of the above wall.

reveal: A set-in at the jamb.

ring stone: Voussoir that shows.

riprap: Stone thrown together without order.

rise: Height of an arch from the middle of the spring line to the bottom of the key stone.

rolled: Construction unit laid with the upper part of its face projecting beyond the plumb line of the wall.

roughly-squared: Stone roughly-squared with a hammer and laid, as in rubble stonework.

rough-pointing: Where a mortar joint is smeared with the trowel, presenting a very messy and rustic mess.

rubble: Unsquared stone, of irregular size and shape.

rule: A measuring tool for distance. Folding rule or measuring tape.

run: Walking space where masons work.

saddle: Apex stone of a gable.

sand: Grains less than 2 millimeters in diameter, commonly of quartz, used as aggregate in mortar.

sandblasting: Engraving, cutting or cleaning with a high velocity stream of sand forcibly projected by air or steam.

sand cushion: Layer of sand separating two structural members, such as subbase and base slab for finished masonry of a floor.

scabbling: Knocking off only the roughest irregularties of a stone.

scaffold: Temporary, movable platform.

scale box: Box for measuring material.

scant: Batter-laid construction unit stepped inward from the plumb line.

screed: A ground of wood, metal or the material being used. It is placed to secure a plumb or level suface.

segmental arch: Shown in arch drawings.

selects: Construction units after culling.

semi-circular arch: Shown in arch drawings.

semi-gothic arch: Shown in arch drawings.

semi-set: Pertains to mortar that has lost its sheen; not hard set.

set: Solidified.

setting coat: Finish coat of plaster and parget.

shell of a chimney: Outside wall of a chimney stack.

shores: Props or temporary under pinning.

shoved joint: Vertical joint made by shoving the bed mortar with the unit being laid; a push joint.

sill: Course or courses of masonry with an inclined face against which voussoirs of an arch abut; a unit placed to receive pressure.

skew corbel: Projecting stone positioned at the bottom or lowest part of a gable top for the purpose of allaying the sliding of the coping.

skintle: To set stone irregularly in a wall so they are out of line with the face of the wall 2 to 3 inches or more.

slaking: Treating lime with water, causing it to heat and crumble.

slope wall: A battered masonry wall out of plumb.

slush joint: Mortar slushed or thrown into a joint with a trowel, not tucked.

smoke chamber: Part of a fireplace, between top of the throat to bottom of the flue.

smoke shelf: Baffle in a flue designed to prevent downdraft.

smooth-pointed: A slicked joint.

sneck: Small roughly-squared stone.

soffit: Underside of a part of a ceiling, overhang or cornice. Intrados of an arch.

spalls: Fragments broken from a stone, and having at least one featherage.

span: Distance of the opening between jambs, abutments, etc.

spandrel: Area between extrados of an arch and adjacent molding or joining arch. The space between the haunch span and right angle.

spirit plumb: Level.

splay: Angle, slope or bend from something, such as the splay from the jamb of a window or door that increases the amount of light through the opening.

spring course: The course an arch springs from, at the skewback unit.

springer: Unit at the impost of an arch. The lowest voussoir of an arch.

spring line: Imaginary line connecting the two opposite points at which the curve of an arch belongs.

spring point: At the spring place from which an arch springs.

square: 90 degree angle corner.

squared: Salient angle or arris of a 90 degree angle presents a squared appearance to a stone, whether the stone has an oblong or square face.

stanchions: Construction units forming the inside angle of a jamb generally made of concrete, which is less costly than dressing or shaping stone.

stock: Construction units, mortar, etc., used in masonry work.

stopped wall: Terminal height of a wall.

story pole: Pole cut to the proposed clear height between finished floor and ceiling, marked with dimensions for courses, sills, frames, string trimmings, etc.

straight arch: Flat arch.

straight edge: Screeding tool or rod of wood or metal which helps secure a grade or straight surface.

string course: Belt course. A projecting or set-out course or courses that extends around a building or across a front.

struck joint: Joint in which green mortar is cut smooth with a trowel.

sunk work: Incised face finish of wrought stone.

superstructure: Structure built as a vertical extension of a building. Structure above the foundation.

tape: An instrument of measurement.

tapping: Pounding a stone to place with a trowel handle, blade or dummy.

tempering: Addition of water to a mix after it has nearly reached or is nearly in its initial set.

template: Gauge or form used as a pattern or copy.

tender: The laborer that tends a stonemason, called a hodman or hod carrier.

tensile/strength: Pertains to the staying together of brickwork. Principally, it is the strength stone or mortar has, and the ability to hold together and not pull apart.

terra-cotta: Glazed or unglazed ceramic building material.

terrazzo: Mosaic surface made by embedding small pieces of marble in mortar and, after hardening, grinding and polishing the surface.

texture: Applied to stone face appearance.

thickness of wall: Distance from face to face through a wall.

throat: Opening in a fireplace from the top of the firebox to the smoke chamber.

throating: Groove on the underside of sills, coping, etc., that prevents water from running back into the wall.

through bond: Tranverse bond formed by a member that extends crosswise through a wall.

through wall: Perpend that extends from face to face through a wall.

throwing mortar: Literally throwing it with the trowel.

tooled: Dressed; reference to smoothing joints.

tools: The necessary instruments used when forming something.

toothing: Alternate courses of stone projecting at the end of a wall to permit bonding into a later continuation of the wall.

trammel: A device for drawing ellipses.

tranverse joint: Joint extending through a wall.

trig: A stone set to the proper height to hold a mason's line level in the center of a course. The line is held in place by a tool called a trig.

trimmer: Beam that receives floor-framing header to keep floor joists away from a chimney.

trimmer arch: Arch built between trimmers in the thickness of an upper floor to support a hearth.

tuck-pointing: Finishing mortar joints with a narrow ridge of putty or fine lime mortar. In tuck-pointing, the old mortar in the joints is routed out to at least ¾ inch and replaced with new mortar near the same color as the construction units in the wall. A grooving tool or jointer is used to indent the new mortar. When the mortar has set sufficiently, it is cut off and trimmed with a trowel.

tying-in: Joining one wall to another.

tympanum: Pedimental space between intrados of a relieving arch and above the lintel or spring line.

vermiculated: Stone dress appearing to be covered with worm tracks.

vertical joint: Cross joint.

vitrification: Fused state by burning.

voids: Air spaces in material.

voussoir: Whole or wedge-shaped unit of an arch placed between a springer unit and the key unit of an arch.

wainscot: Lower 3 or 4 feet of an interior wall when finished differently from the rest of the wall.

wall plate: First member above a wall and on which the roof is laid.

wall ties: Mortar-embedded ties that hold walls or units together.

wash: Slope given stone to shed water.

washing: Cleaning stonework with a liquid solution.

water joint: Raised tooled mortar joint, generally a floor joint, which will drain off water.

water table: Course near the base of a structure, projecting to throw off water.

weathering: Decay or deterioration by the effects of the elements of nature.

weep hole: Hole left mortar-free in masonry that will drain off water.

wind shelf: Smoke shelf.

wing wall: Extended abutment to retain earth.

withe: The partition between flues in the same chimney.

wrought: Shaping of a stone ready for setting.

Appendix A
Tables of Weights
and Measures

There are two dominant systems used to measure quantity: United States and metric. The United States system is employed in all measurements in this book. Should the need arise, a change over to metric system is possible with the use of the following information and tables.

The United States system listed in Tables A-1 through A-3 shows the units of measure regarding length, area, capacity and weight. Each unit has its own measure of value. Such value may be changed to metric equivalents (Tables A-4 through A-9). Measures and weights of material supplies are given in Tables A-10 and A-11 Table A-12 lists circular measures.

TEMPERATURE CONVERSIONS

It is also necessary to watch the temperature. Mortars should not freeze or stonework is worthless. Since there are two tempera-

Table A-1. Units of distance measure in the
United States system and their abbreviations.

U.S. SYSTEM: DESIGNATIONS AND ABBREVIATIONS		
Unit Name	Area (Square)	Quantity (Cubic)
inch (in.)	square inch (sq. in.)	cubic inch (cu. in.)
foot (ft.)	square foot (sq. ft.)	cubic foot (cu. ft.)
yard (yd.)	square yard (sq. yd.)	cubic yard (cu. yd.)
rod (rd.)	square rod (sq. rd.)	cubic rod (cu. rd.)
mile (mi.)	square mile (sq. mi.)	cubic mile (cu. mi.)

Table A-2. Units of capacity measure in the American system and their abbreviations.

CAPACITY UNIT MEASURES		
gill (gi.) pt.	quart (qt.) peck (pk.)	gallon (gal.) bushel (bu.)

Table A-3. Units of weight measure in the
United States system and their abbreviations.

WEIGHT UNIT MEASURES		
grain (gr.) pound (lb.) hundredweight (cwt.)	dram (dr.) fluid oz. (fl. oz.) short ton (s. t.)	ounce (oz.) dry oz. (dry oz.) long ton (l. t.)

Table A-4. Units of length, capacity and weight
measure in the metric system, together with abbreviations.

METRIC ABBREVIATIONS AND SYMBOLS	
Length Measure	Square Measure
millimeter (mm.) centimeter (cm.) decimeter (dm.) meter (m.) decimeter (dkm.) hectometer (hm.) kilometer (km.)	square millimeter (sq. mm.) square centimeter (sq. cm.) square decimeter (sq. dm.) square meter (sq. m.) square decimeter (sq. dkm.) square hectometer (sq. hm.) square kilometer (sq. km.)

Cubic Measure	Capacity
cubic millimeter (cu. mm.) cubic centimeter (cu. cm.) cubic decimeter (cu. dm.) cubic meter (cu. m.) cubic decameter (cu. dkm.) cubic hectometer (cu. hm.) cubic kilometer (cu. km.)	milliliter (ml.) centiliter (cl.) deciliter (dl.) liter (l.) decaliter (dkl.) hectoliter (hl.) kiloliter (kl.)

Weight Measure	Weight Measure
milligram (mg.) centigram (cg.) decigram (dg.) gram (g.)	decagram (dkg.) hectogram (hg.) kilogram (kg.) metric ton (M.T.)

266

Table A-5. American units of length measure changed to metric equivalents.

U.S. UNITS OF MEASURE CHANGED TO METRIC EQUIVALENTS		
Units of Length	U.S. System	Metric System
inch (in.)	0.083 ft.	25.4 mm.; 2.54 cm.
foot (ft.)	12 in.⅓ yd.	30.48 cm.; 0.3048 m.
yard (yd.)	36 in.; 3 ft.	0.9144 m.
rod (rd.)	16½ ft.; 5 ½ yd.	5.0292 m.
land mile (mi.)	1760 yd.; 5280 ft.	1609.344 m.
Nautical mile	1.151 land mile	1.852 km.
sq. in.	0.007 sq. ft.	6.4516 sq. cm.
sq. ft.	144 sq. in.	929.030 sq. cm.
sq. yd.	1296 sq. in.; 9 sq. ft.	0.8361 sq. m.
sq. acre; (sq. A.)	43,560 sq. ft.	4.047 sq. m.
sq. mi.	640 Acres	2.590 sq. km.
cu. in.	0.00058 cu. ft.	16.387 cu. cm.
cu. ft.	1728 cu. in.	0.028 cu. m.
cu. yd.	27 cu. ft.	0.765 cu. m.

Table A-6. United States units of weight measure and their metric equivalents.

WEIGHT MEASURE		
Units of Weight	U.S. System	Metric
gr.	0.036 dr.; 0.002285 oz.	64.79891 mg.
dr.	27.344 gr.; 0.0625 oz.	1.772 gr.
oz.	16 dr.; 437.5 gr.	28.350 gr.
lb.	16 oz.; 7000 gr.	453.59237 gr.
s. t.	2000 lb.	0.907 M.T.
l. t.	1.12 s.t.; 2240 lb.	1.016 M. T.

Table A-7. American units of capacity measure and metric equivalents.

CAPACITY MEASURE		
Units of Capacity	U.S. System	Metric
f. oz. (liquid)	8 fl. dr.; 1.804 cu. in.	29.573 ml.
pt. "	1 fl. oz.; 528.875 cu. in.	0.473 l.
qt. "	2 pt.; 57.75 cu. in.	0.946 l.
gal. "	4 qt.; 231 cu. in.	3.785 l.
bbl. "	31 to 42 gal. (180 lb. U.S.)	81.65 kg.
pt. dry	½ qt.; 33.6 cu. in.	0.551 l.
qt. "	2 pt.; 67.2 cu. in.	1.101 l.
pk. "	8 qt.; 537.606 cu. in	8.810 l.
bu. "	4 pk.; 2150.42 cu. in.	35.2381 l.

Table A-8. British units of liquid and dry capacity measure.

oz.	0.961 U.S. fl. oz. 1.734 cu. in.	28.413 ml.
pt.	1.032 U.S. dry pt. 1.201 U.S. fl. pt. 34.678 cu. in.	568.26 ml.
qt.	1.032 U.S. dry qt. 1.201 U.S. fl. qt.	1.136 l.
pk.	554.84 cu. in.	0.009 cu. m.
bu.	1.032 U.S. bu. 2.219.36 cu. in.	0.036 m.

Table A-9. Metric units of measure and their American equivalents.

mm.	0.03937 in.	0.00328 ft.
cm.	0.3937 in.	0.0328 ft.
dm.	3.937 in.	0.328 ft.
m.	39.37 in.	3.28 ft.
dkm.	393.7 in.	32.8 ft.
dm.	3937 in.	328 ft.
km.	0.621 mi.	3280.8 ft.

Table A-10. Measures and weights of materials.

MEASURES AND WEIGHTS OF MATERIAL SUPPLIES (Approximately)		
1 cu. ft.	water	62.4 lbs.
1 gal.	muriatic acid	9+ lbs.
1 bucket (12 qt.)	lime putty	30 lbs.
1 bucket (12 qt.)	hydrated lime	16 lbs.
1 bucket (12 qt.)	Keene's cement	30 lbs.
1 bucket (12 qt.)	sand	40 lbs.
1 bushel (4 pk.) bu.	Portland cement	126 lbs.
1 bu.	slaked quicklime putty	100 lbs.
1 bu.	hydrated lime putty	109 lbs.
1 bu.	hydrated lime	50 lbs.
1 bu.	quicklime	72 lbs.
1 bu.	Keene's cement	94 lbs.
1 T.	clay	16 cu. ft.
1 T.	sand	18 to 22 cu. ft.
1 cu. yd.	sand (dry)	2500 to 2700 lbs.
1 bag (1 cu. ft.)	Portland cement	94 lbs.
1 bag	hydrated lime	50 lbs.
1 bbl.	cement	376 lbs.
1 bbl.	quicklime	180 lbs.
1 cu. ft.	hydrated lime	40 lbs.
1 cu. ft.	lime	45 lbs.
1 cu. ft.	hydrated lime putty	83 lbs.
1 cu. ft.	lime putty	2.7 bucket (12 qt.)

Table A-11. Cubic foot weight of selected materials.

Loose dirt	90 to 100 lbs.	Limestone	170 to 184 lbs.
Clay and gravel	300 lbs.	Random and split ashlar stone	160 lbs.
Sand	90 to 113 lbs.	Sandstone	140 to 144 lbs.
New Mortar	115 lbs.	Granite	160 to 172 lbs.
Old Mortar	90 lbs.	Marble	168 to 174 lbs.
Quick Lime	58 lbs.	Loadstone	305 lbs.
Cement Mortar	112 lbs.	Slate	166 lbs.
Portland Cement	94 lbs.	Rubble	130 lbs.
Hydrated Lime	40 lbs.	Common Stone	158 lbs.
Gypsum	143 lbs.	Quartz	166 lbs.
Tar	64 lbs.	Portland Stone	157 lbs.
Asbestos	188 lbs.	Porcelain Stone	159 lbs.
Cork	15 lbs.	Brick	119 to 128 lbs.
Asphalt	103 lbs.		

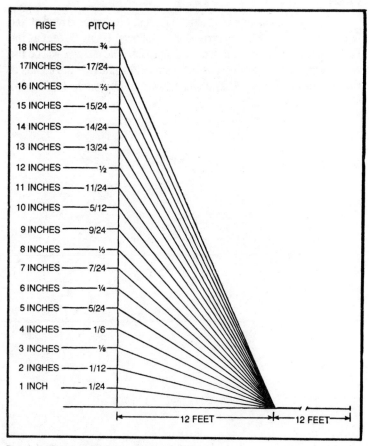

Fig. A-1. This graph shows rise and pitch.

1 minute (')	60 seconds (")
1 degree (°)	60', 1 °
1 circle	360°

Table A-12. Units of circular measure.

ture thermometers, the Fahrenheit and the Centigrade, it may become necessary to convert the scale reading from one to the other.

To convert the Fahrenheit reading to the Centigrade, take 32 from the Fahrenheit reading and multiply by five-ninths. The answer is Centigrade temperature reading.

To convert the Centigrade reading to the Fahrenheit temperature reading, take the Centigrade reading times five-ninths, and add 32. The answer will be Farenheit reading.

PITCH

The various slopes of roofs, wall tops, etc., are arrived at and figured in pitches. Pitch is arrived at as follows. Using 24 feet as the base (width), divide the pitch desired into 24. The answer will be the rise in inches. Using 24 feet as the base (width), divide the inches of the rise desired into 24. The answer will be the pitch. Figure A-1 shows rise and pitch.

Appendix B

Table B-1 Recommended maximum permissible
water-cement ratios for different types of structures and degrees of exposure.

Type of structure	Exposure conditions**					
	Severe wide range in temperature or frequenct alternations of freezing and thawing (air-entrained concrete only) (gallons/sack)			Mild temperature rarely below freezing, or rainy, or arid (gallons/sack)		
	In air	At water line or within range of fluctuating water level or spray		In air	At water line or within range of fluctuating water level or spray	
		In fresh water	In sea water or in contact with sulfatest†		In fresh water	In sea water or in contact with sulfatest††
A. Thin sections such as reinforced piles and pipe	5.5	5	4.5	6	5.5	4.5
B. Bridge decks	5	5	4.5	5.5	5.5	5
C. Thin sections such as railings, curbs, sills, ledges, ornamental or architectural concrete, and all sections with less than 1-in. concrete cover over reinforcement	5.5	......	......	6	5.5	......
D. Moderate sections, such as retaining walls, abutments, piers, girders, beams	6	5.5	5	††	6	5
E. Exterior portions of heavy (mass) sections	6.5	5.5	5	††	6	5

F. Concrete deposited by tremie under water	.5	5	5	5
G. Concrete slabs laid on the ground	6	......	......	......
H. Pavements	5.5	......	......	......
I. Concrete protected from the weather, interiors of buildings, concrete below ground	††	††	6	......
J. Concrete which will later be protected by enclosure or backfill but which may be exposed to freezing and thawing for several years before such protection is offered	6	††	......	......

*Adapted from Recommended Practice for Selecting Proportions for Concrete (ACI 613-54).

**Air-entrained concrete should be used under all conditions involving severe exposure and may be used under mild exposure conditions to improve workability of the mixture.

†Soil or groundwater containing sulfate concentrations of more than 0.2 per cent. For moderate sulfate resistance, the tricaleium aluminate content of the cement should be limited to 8 per cent, and for high sulfate resistance to 5 percent. At equal cement contents, air-entrained concrete is significantly more resistant to sulfate attack than non-air-entrained concrete.

††Water-cement ratio should be selected on basis of strength and workability requirements, but minimum cement content should not be less than 470 lbs. per cubic yard.

Table B-2. Age and compressive strength relationship
for types I and III air-entrained Portland cement (continued on pages 275 through 277).

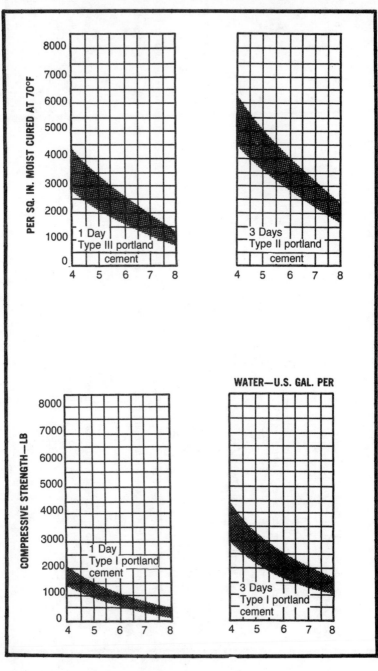

Table B-2. Portland cement (continued on page 276).

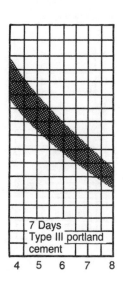

7 Days
Type III portland cement

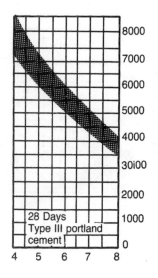

28 Days
Type III portland cement

8000
7000
6000
5000
4000
30i00
2000
1000
0

SACK OF CEMENT

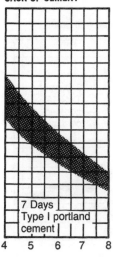

7 Days
Type I portland cement

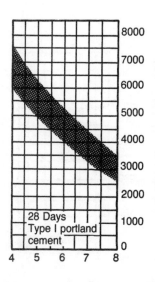

28 Days
Type I portland cement

8000
7000
6000
5000
4000
3000
2000
1000
0

275

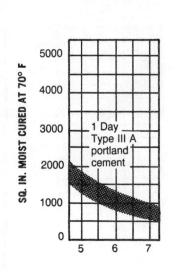

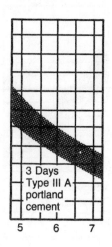

WATER U.S. GAL. PER SACK

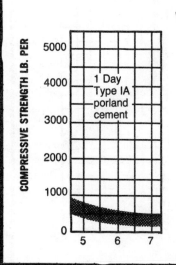

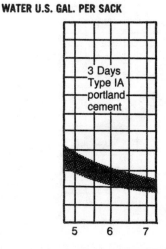

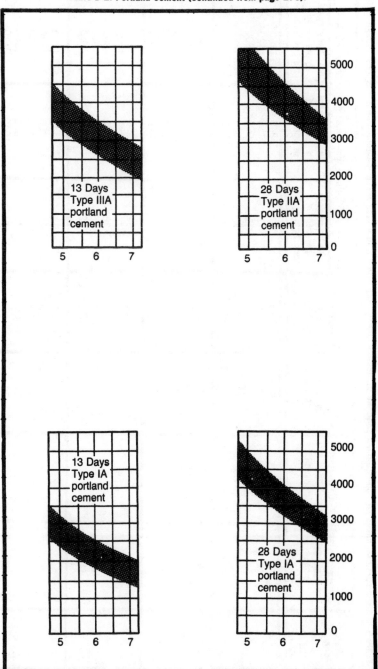

Table B-3. Suggested trial mixes for non-entrained concrete of medium consistency with a 3 to 4-inch slump (continued on pages 279 through 281).

Water-cement ratio Gal per sack	Maximum size of aggregate inches	Air content (entrapped air) per cent	Water gal per cu yd of concrete	Cement sacks per cu yd of concrete	With fine sand—fineness modulus = 2.50		
					Fine aggregate per cent of total aggregate	Fine aggregate lb per cu yd of concrete	Coarse aggregate lb per cu yd of concrete
4.5	3/8	3	46	10.3	50	1240	1260
	1/2	2.5	44	9.8	42	1100	1520
	3/4	2	41	9.1	35	960	1800
	1	1.5	39	8.7	32	910	1940
	1½	1	36	8.0	29	880	2110
5.0	3/8	3	46	9.2	51	1330	1260
	1/2	2.5	44	8.8	44	1130	1520
	3/4	2	41	8.2	37	1040	1800
	1	1.5	39	7.8	34	990	1940
		1	36	7.2	31	960	2110
5.5	3/8	3	46	8.4	52	1390	1260
	1/2	2.5	44	8.0	45	1240	1520
	3/4	2	41	7.5	38	1090	1800
	1	1.5	39	7.1	35	1040	1940
	1½	1	36	6.5	32	1000	2110
6.0	3/8	3	46	7.7	53	1440	1260
	1/2	2.5	44	7.3	46	1290	1520
	3/4	2	41	6.8	39	1130	1800
	1	1.5	39	6.5	36	1080	1940
	1½	1	36		32	1040	2110

6.5	3/8	3	46	7.1	54	1480	1260
	1/2	2.5	44	6.8	46	1320	1520
	3/4	2	41	6.3	39	1190	1800
	1	1.5	39	6.0	37	1120	1940
	1½	1	36	5.5	34	1070	2110
7.0	3/8	3	46	6.6	55	1520	1260
	1/2	2.5	44	6.3	47	1360	1520
	3/4	2	41	5.9	40	1200	1800
	1	1.5	39	5.6	37	1150	1940
	1½	1	36	5.1	34	1100	2110
7.5	3/8	3	46	6.1	55	1560	1260
	1/2	2.5	44	5.9	48	1400	1520
	3/4	2	41	5.5	41	1240	1800
	1	1.5	39	5.2	38	1190	1940
	1½	1	36	4.8	35	1130	2110
8.0	3/8	3	46	5.7	56	1600	1260
	1/2	2.5	44	5.5	48	1440	1520
	3/4	2	41	5.1	42	1230	1800
	1	1.5	39	4.9	39	1220	1940
	1½	1	36	4.5	35	1160	2110

Table B-3. Trial mixes (continued from page 279 and on page 281).

Water-cement ratio Gal per sack	With average sand—fineness modulus = 2.75			With coarse sand—fineness modulus = 2.90		
	Fine aggregate percent of total aggregate	Fine aggregate lb per cu yd of concrete	Coarse aggregate lb per cu yd of concrete	Fine aggregate percent of total aggregate	Fine aggregate lb per cu yd of concrete	Coarse aggregate lb per cu yd of concrete
4.5	52	1310	1190	54	1350	1150
	45	1170	1450	47	1220	1400
	37	1030	1730	39	1080	1680
	34	980	1870	36	1020	1830
	32	960	2030	33	1000	1990
5.0	54	1400	1190	56	1440	1150
	46	1250	1450	48	1300	1400
	39	1110	1730	41	1160	1680
	36	1060	1870	38	1100	1830
	34	1040	2030	35	1080	1990
5.5	55	1460	1190	57	1500	
	47	1310	1450	49	1360	
	40	1160	1730	42	1210	
	37	1110	1870	39	1150	
	35	1080	2030	36	1120	
6.0	56	1510	1190	57	1550	1150
	48	1360	1450	50	1410	1400
	41	1200	1730	43	1250	1600
	38	1150	1870	39	1190	1830
	36	1120	2030	37	1160	1990

Slump	%			%		
6.5	57	1550	1190	58	1590	1150
	49	1390	1450	51	1440	1400
	42	1240	1730	43	1290	1680
	39	1190	1870	40	1230	1830
	36	1150	2030	37	1190	1990
7.0	57	1590	1190	59	1630	1150
	50	1430	1450	51	1480	1400
	42	1270	1730	44	1320	1680
	39	1220	1870	41	1260	1830
	37	1180	2030	38	1220	1990
7.5	58	1630	1190	59	1670	1150
	50	1470	1450	52	1520	1400
	43	1310	1730	45	1370	1600
	40	1260	1870	42	1300	1830
	37	1210	2030	39	1250	1990
8.0	58	1670	1190	60	1710	1150
	51	1520	1450	53	1560	1400
	44	1350	1730	45	1400	1680
	41	1290	1870	42	1330	1830
	38	1250	2030	39	1280	1990

*Increase or decrease water per cubic yard by 3 per cent for each increase or decrease of 1 in. in slump, then calculate quantities by absolute volume method. For manufactured fine aggregate, increase percentage of fine aggregate by 3 and water by 17 lb. per cubic yard of concrete. For less workable concrete, as in pavements decrease percentage of fine aggregate by 3 and water by 8 lb. per cubic yard of concrete.

Table B-4. Trial mixes for air-entrained concrete of medium consistency with a 3 to 4-inch slump (continued on pages 283 through 285).

Water-cement ratio Gal per sack	Maximum size of aggregate inches	Air Content (entrapped air) per cent	Water gal per cu yd of concrete	Cement sacks per cu yd of concrete	With fine sand—fineness modulus = 2.50		
					Fine aggregate per cent of total aggregate	Fine aggregate lb per cu yd of concrete	Coarse aggregate lb per cu yd of concrete
4.5	3/8	7.5	41	9.1	50	1250	1260
	1/2	7.5	39	8.7	41	1060	1520
	3/4	6	36	8.0	35	970	1800
	1	6	34	7.8	32	900	1940
	1½	5	32	7.1	29	870	2110
5.0	3/8	7.5	41	8.2	51	1330	1260
	1/2	7.5	39	7.8	43	1140	1520
	3/4	6	36	7.2	37	1040	1800
	1	6	34	6.8	33	970	1940
	1½	5	32	6.4	31	930	2110
5.5	3/8	7.5	41	7.5	52	1390	1260
	1/2	7.5	39	7.1	44	1190	1520
	3/4	6	36	6.5	38	1090	1800
	1	6	34	6.2	34	1010	1940
	1½	5	32	5.8	32	970	2110
6.0	3/8	7.5	41	6.8	53	1430	1260
	1/2	7.5	39	6.5	45	1230	1520
	3/4	6	36	6.0	38	1120	1800
	1	6	34	5.7	35	1040	1940
	1½	5	32	5.3	32	1010	2110

6.5	3⁄8	7.5	41	6.3	54	1460	1260
	1⁄2	7.5	39	6.0	45	1260	1520
	1⁄2	6	36	5.5	39	1150	1800
	1	6	34	5.2	36	1080	1940
	1 1⁄2	5	32	4.9	33	1040	2110
7.0	3⁄8	7.5	41	5.9	54	1500	1260
	1⁄2	7.5	39	5.6	46	1300	1520
	3⁄4	6	36	5.1	40	1180	1800
	1	6	34	4.9	36	1100	1940
	1 1⁄2	5	32	4.6	33	1060	2110
7.5	3⁄8	7.5	41	5.5	55	1530	1260
	1⁄2	7.5	39	5.2	47	1330	1520
	3⁄4	6	36	4.8	40	1210	1800
	1	6	34	4.5	37	1140	1940
	1 1⁄2	5	32	4.3	34	1090	2110
8.0	3⁄8	7.5	41	5.1	55	1560	1260
	1⁄2	7.5	39	4.9	47	1360	1520
	3⁄4	6	36	4.5	41	1240	1800
	1	6	34	4.3	37	1160	1940
	1 1⁄2	5	32	4.0	34	1110	2110

Table B-4. Trial mixes (continued from page 283 and continued on page 284).

Water-cement ratio Gal per sack	With average sand—fineness modulus = 2.75			With coarse sand—fineness modulus = 2.90		
	Fine aggregate percent of total aggregate	Fine aggregate lb per cu yd of concrete	Coarse aggregate lb per cu yd of concrete	Fine aggregate percent of total aggregate	Fine aggregate lb per cu yd of concrete	Coarse aggregate lb per cu yd of concrete
4.5	53	1320	1190	54	1360	1150
	44	1130	1450	46	1180	1400
	38	1040	1730	39	1090	1680
	34	970	1870	36	1010	1830
	32	950	2030	33	990	1990
5.0	54	1400	1190	56	1440	1150
	46	1210	1450	47	1260	1400
	39	1110	1730	41	1160	1630
	36	1040	1870	37	1080	1830
	33	1010	2030	35	1050	1990
5.5	55	1460	1190	57	1500	1150
	46	1260	1450	48	1310	1400
	40	1160	1730	42	1210	1680
	37	1080	1870	38	1120	1830
	34	1050	2030	35	1090	1990
6.0	56	1500	1190	57	1540	1150
	47	1300	1450	49	1350	1400
	41	1190	1730	42	1240	1680
	37	1110	1870	39	1150	1830
	35	1090	2030	36	1130	1990

6.5	56	1530	1190	58	1570	1150
	48	1330	1450	50	1380	1400
	41	1220	1730	43	1270	1680
	38	1150	1870	39	1190	1830
	36	1120	2030	37	1160	1990
7.0	57	1570	1190	58	1610	1150
	49	1370	1450	50	1420	1400
	42	1250	1730	44	1300	1680
	38	1170	1870	40	1210	1830
	36	1140	2030	37	1180	1990
7.5	57	1600	1190	59	1640	1150
	49	1400	1450	51	1450	1400
	43	1280	1730	44	1330	1680
	39	1210	1870	41	1250	1830
	37	1170	2030	38	1210	1990
8.0	58	1630	1190	59	1670	1150
	50	1430	1450	51	1480	1400
	43	1310	1730	44	1360	1680
	40	1230	1870	41	1270	1830
	37	1190	2030	38	1230	1990

*Increase or decrease water per cubic yard by 3 per cent for each increase of 1 in. in slump, then calculate quantities by absolute volume method. For manufactured fine aggregate, increase percentage of fine aggregate by 3 and water by 17 lb. per cubic yard of concrete. For less workable concrete, as in pavements decrease percentage of fine aggregate by 3 and water by 8 lb. per cubic yard of concrete.

Table B-5. Approximate mixing water requirements
for different slumps and maximum sizes of aggregates.

Maximum size of aggregate, in.	Air-entrained concrete				Approximate amount of entrapped air, per cent	Non-air-entrained concrete		
	Recommended average total air content, per cent×	Slump, in.				Slump, in.		
		1 to 2	3 to 4	5 to 6		1 to 2	3 to 4	5 to 6
		Water, gal. per cu. yd. of conctete*				Water, gal. per cu. yd. of concrete**		
3/8	7.5	37	41	43	3.0	42	46	49
1/2	7.5	36	39	41	2.5	40	44	46
3/4	6.0	33	36	38	2.0	37	41	43
1	6.0	31	34	36	1.5	36	39	41
1½	5.0	29	32	34	1.0	33	36	38
2	5.0	27	30	32	0.5	31	34	36
3	4.0	25	28	30	0.3	29	32	34
6	3.0	22	24	26	0.2	25	28	30

*Adapted from Recommended Practice for Selecting Proportions for Concrete (ACI 613-54).
**These quantities of mixing water are for use in computing cement factors for trial batches. They are maximums for reasonably well-shaped angular coarse aggregates graded within limits of accepted specifications.
†Plus or minus 1 per cent.

Table B-6. Details of common nails.

PENNY SIZE	LENGTH (INCHES)	GAGE	NUMBER PER POUND
2	1	155	840
3	1¼	14	540
4	1½	12½	300
6	2	11½	160
8	2½	10¼	100
10	3	9	65
12	3¼	9	65
16	3½	8	45
20	4	6	30
30	4½	5	20
40	5	4	17
50	5¼	3	14
60	6	2	11

Index